SAINT
ANTHONY
and
SAINT
JUDE

SAINT
ANTHONY
and
SAINT
JUDE

TRUE STORIES OF HEAVENLY HELP

Mitch Finley

Liguori

LIGUORI, MISSOURI

Published by Liguori Publications
Liguori, Missouri
www.liguori.org
www.catholicbooksonline.com

This book is a revised edition of *Heavenly Helpers: St. Anthony and St. Jude* published in 1994 by The Crossroad Publishing Company, New York, New York.

Library of Congress Cataloging-in-Publication Data

Finley, Mitch.
    Saint Anthony and Saint Jude : true stories of heavenly help Mitch Finley.
        p.   cm.
    Rev. ed. of: Heavenly helpers. 1994.
    ISBN 0-7648-0783-8 (pbk.)
    1. Anthony, of Padua, Saint, 1195–1231. 2. Jude, Saint. 3. Anthony of Padua, Saint 1195–1231—Prayer-books and devotions—English. 4. Jude, Saint—Prayer-books and devotions—English. I. Finley, Mitch. Heavenly helpers. II. Title.

BX4700.A6 F56   2001
235'.2—dc21   2001033451

Printed in the United States of America
05 04 03 02 01   5 4 3 2 1
Revised edition 2001

CONTENTS

ACKNOWLEDGMENTS

I owe a debt of gratitude to the hundreds of people who took the time to write their stories and send them to me. Equal thanks are due the many editors who published my letter in their magazine or newspaper inviting people to send me their stories.

FOREWORD

For those people who have a devotion to Saint Anthony or Saint Jude—or better yet, those people seeking to foster such a devotion—Mitch Finley's *Saint Anthony and Saint Jude: True Stories of Heavenly Help* is a resource par excellence. It is "heavenly help" at your fingertips.

As a child, I grew up in a family that had great devotion to these two saints. My mother had a personal relationship with Saint Anthony. Her confidence in this wonder-worker and finder of lost items was as easy and unassuming as apple pie and homemade bread. Her devotion was more like a friendship, and I grew up with a devotion to Saint Anthony as a part of my early spiritual development. He was a friend and helper to my family. My memory is filled with many experiences of prayers answered by this loving saint, and even to this day I find myself saying a prayer to Saint Anthony every now and then.

And then there's Saint Jude. Next door to my childhood home there lived a woman who was eager to tell everyone about Saint Jude and how he was the one to go to when you were at the end of your wits with worry and anxiety. She had personal experience in her own life with some miraculous events involving family members who found themselves rescued from desperate circumstances after petitioning the saint to intercede on their behalf. So we all knew why the large statue of Saint Jude stood in the center of her beautiful garden.

It is timely that this book has reappeared on the publishing map in its revised form. There is a new and growing inter-

est in these two saints and their intercessory power. Many
people are looking for a resource that encourages them in
their devotion. Mitch Finley's book can fulfill this need. In
this fine work, one can find a simple rendering of the lives of
these two saints, how Saints Anthony and Jude became known
for their miraculous intervention. Mitch Finley deftly presents
the tradition of devotion to the saints in its proper context,
addressing those unhealthy misconceptions of devotion that
give an impression of "magic" in regard to saintly intercession.

This revised publication of *Heavenly Helpers* contains new
letters witnessing to the miraculous intervention of Saint Anthony and Saint Jude. The letters are an inspiration to all
who are in need of encouragement and hope. The addition of
the novenas and prayers at the end of the book lend a devotional and practical quality to the work as a whole.

Those who are already devotees to Saint Anthony or Saint
Jude will find this book a welcome and encouraging resource
that they will want to have for their daily devotional life. For
those who have heard about the power of these "Helpers of
Those in Need," and who wish to know more about who
these saints are, what they have done, and ways to petition
their intercession through prayer, will find all they need in
Saint Anthony and Saint Jude: True Stories of Heavenly Help.

I applaud Mitch Finley for providing this resource in light
of the growing interest in prayers and devotions that are the
heritage of our Catholic tradition. In these times of devotional renaissance, there is a need for presenting to Catholics
the best of our age-old wealth of devotions and prayers.

May Saint Anthony and Saint Jude continue to be the
"heavenly helpers" of all who call upon them.

BROTHER DANIEL KORN, C.SS.R.
DIRECTOR OF DEVOTIONS IN HONOR OF
OUR MOTHER OF PERPETUAL HELP AND
SAINT GERARD MAJELLA

INTRODUCTION
Their Purpose Is Love

T here is more to life and the world than what meets the eye, and I don't mean subatomic particles and the astonishments of quantum physics. You and I live spiritual cheek by spiritual jowl with people who once thrashed around in the here and now as we do, but no longer. They are right over there—as eternity is—just beyond our vision. They are so close that you would jump a foot in the air if you could see them. They are people who "passed over," who—to use our dark word—*died*. Yet the life they enjoy is far more lively than mere biological percolation.

These people, who live "eternally," care about us, and they are so intimate with the Divine Mystery that they cannot but act in loving concord with the Divine Will. When we speak to them, they hear us, and they respond to our cares and concerns even in the most trivial, everyday matters. Two of these people, for reasons hidden in the Divine Purpose, occupy a special place in the lives of countless Christians. Their names are Anthony of Padua and Jude Thaddeus, sometimes called "the Obscure." Anthony and Jude help people by their eternal communion with the Divine. That is their purpose, and their purpose is love.

The Communion of Saints

Since the days of the early Christians—and since the fifth century in the Apostles' Creed—those who follow Christ have held a belief in "the communion of saints." This idea came from the New Testament concept of *koinonia* (community), the fellowship in faith shared by all believers with the risen Christ. "Saints" is used here as Saint Paul uses it in his letters, meaning all the people of God who are one in their shared faith. (See, for example, 1 Corinthians 1:2.) The "saints" pray for one another and help one another. This union among the "saints" continues among both the living and those who live that better life called "eternal."

Since the earliest centuries, Christians believed that it is possible for people of faith who died to help, by their prayers, those still on pilgrimage through time and space. Thus, Christians of the Roman Catholic, Eastern Orthodox, and—to a lesser extent—Anglican traditions feel free to ask deceased relatives and friends to pray for them.

Among the early Christians, veneration of martyrs for the faith was a communal activity. *Newsweek* religion editor Kenneth L. Woodward explains in *Making Saints*: "Whatever else it entailed, veneration of the saints was a liturgical act. Saints were remembered, invoked, prayed to wherever Christians assembled for worship."

On a more formal level, "canonized" saints—those declared worthy of public veneration either by popular acclamation (in the early centuries) or by church authorities (since about the twelfth century)—attracted a popular devotion that often transcends locality, culture, and historical time and place. For reasons human and/or divine, various canonized saints, including the two this book concerns itself with, became more popular than others. These saints captured the popular imagination by the power of their image, the stories about their lives, and—let us accept the possibility—by answering prayers more reliably than their heavenly peers.

Christian doctrine does not and never has held that the veneration of saints is "necessary for salvation." On the contrary. Still, the veneration of saints has historical and scriptural roots. "The early Christians revered the Blessed Virgin and the martyrs," say Gerald O'Collins, S.J., and Edward G. Farrugia, S.J., in *A Concise Dictionary of Theology*. The Letter to the Hebrews (11:1—12:1) lists many heroes and heroines of faith from the Hebrew Scriptures or Old Testament. "Origen (ca. 185–254) was the first to reflect seriously on devotion to the saints. The first nonmartyrs to be venerated were Saint Antony the Abbot (ca. 251–356) and Saint Martin of Tours (d. 397)."

Why Pray to Saints?

Clearly, the veneration of saints goes back to the earliest Christian communities. Still, there are many today who reject the idea not only for themselves—which they have every right to do—but for anyone else, as well. For such people, the veneration of saints is virtual heresy. "I used to pray to Saint Jude and other saints," says Andrew R., of Bellmore, New York, in a letter I received along with those from which the stories in this book come. "Then," he continued, "I read the Bible and prayed directly to Jesus.... People are being deceived by hundred-year-old traditions of praying to saints. Why would you need to if you have Jesus?"

For nearly two thousand years, Christians have honored and prayed to saints because they see in them God's self-gift, or grace, at work in special ways. Since the Protestant Reformation in the mid-sixteenth century, most Protestants have rejected the veneration of saints. Yet we may ask, Why should people stop praying for one another after they die? Does it not stand to reason that someone who manifested the love of

God in special ways in this world would pray for us even after crossing the Great Divide? To pray to saints does not detract from faith in Christ but does him honor by honoring the power of his love at work in the saints.

To pray to a saint is to address oneself to the power and grace of God active in a human being who now enjoys eternal life. Just as God works through our prayers for one another in this world, God works through our prayers to saints and through their prayers for us. In 1964, the Catholic Church's Second Vatican Council declared that "our communion with those in heaven, provided that it is understood in the full light of faith, in no way diminishes the worship of adoration given to God the Father, through Christ, in the Spirit; on the contrary, it greatly enriches it" (Dogmatic Constitution on the Church, art. 51).

There comes a point in the attempt to understand all this when the human mind reaches its limits. There is a tremendous mystery here. Ultimately, the love of God is active in us and in the saints, and we are at a loss to grasp fully how it works. From the days of the earliest Christians, believers grasped with their heart that their relationships with those who died in the faith were not ended but transformed. They are still with us, in a marvelous but mysterious way, and they can help us by their prayers. Countless ordinary Christians who pray to Saint Jude, Saint Anthony, or another saint take it for granted that he or she prays to the saint for the saint's "intercession." People of faith venerate—respect or reverence—the saints, they do not worship them. Such people reject the suggestion that the saint has power independent of the power of God.

"We, the Christian community," wrote Saint Augustine in the fifth century, "assemble to celebrate the memory of the martyrs with ritual solemnity because we want to be inspired to follow their example, share in their merits, and be helped by their prayers....

"But the veneration strictly called worship, *latria*, that is, the special homage belonging only to divinity, is something we give and teach others to give to God alone."

The Christian faith, as lived for nearly two thousand years, includes participation in the communion of saints. To have friends both in this world and in eternity is to belong to a faith community that is both immediate and transcendent. That is what people do who have heavenly friends and helpers—including Mary, the mother of Jesus, Saint Anthony, Saint Teresa of Ávila, Saint Jude, Saint Francis of Assisi, Saint Thérèse of Lisieux, and many others. Just as we sometimes rely on the love of our friends in this world, so we may rely on the love of our friends in the next world. Their love is God's love, "for God is love" (1 John 4:8).

Some Slip Over the Edge

It is possible to abuse any good. It is possible to distort any truth into a falsehood. Thus, you will find people who relate to saints in clearly un-Christian, unhealthy ways. The technical meaning of "magic" is to try to control transcendent forces by the use of certain words and/or rituals. Some people believe that if you say a certain prayer a certain number of times to a certain saint, marvelous results are guaranteed. This is a magical approach to the veneration of saints, and it is sheer religious flapdoodle.

Reading this book, you will notice that people sometimes use the term "novena." A novena is a traditional Christian approach to prayer. Correctly understood, all it means is to pray for nine consecutive days—from the Latin for nine, *novum*—for a specific intention. The idea of praying for nine days comes straight from the New Testament, from the account of the nine days of prayer by the disciples and Mary between Ascension and Pentecost, in the Acts of the Apostles (1:9, 13, and 2:1).

There is nothing magical about the number nine, or about saying a particular prayer for nine days. But it takes persistence to say a prayer nine days in a row, and so a novena is one response to the admonition of Jesus to be persistent in prayer and "to not lose heart" (Luke 18:1). When someone "makes a novena" to Saint Anthony or Saint Jude, the goal is not to do something magical, but to keep on praying and not give up. By extension, a novena may last for any length of time.

In some of the stories you will read here, people say that they promised Saint Anthony or Saint Jude to make a donation of money to a charitable organization, or "to the poor" if the saint would help them. Others promise to give up something, such as candy or "junk food," or to light a candle in honor of the saint. This may sound like spiritual bribery, but perhaps not. To promise to give away money is to promise to take a tangible step toward being less dependent on money and more dependent on God. It can be a promise to do something to help others. To light a candle can be a promise to dedicate oneself to a deeper prayer life; to give up junk food can be a commitment to respect one's body more. Ideally, the purpose is not to "bribe" the saint but to become less self-centered, a bit more focussed on the needs of others—in one way or another, to become a more faith-centered person. It can be a way to express gratitude by sharing one's gifts with those who have less.

Why Don't Saint Anthony and Saint Jude Always Come Through?

You will read many inspiring stories in this book, some telling of dramatic cures or astonishing cases of lost things found. All come from the people who lived the stories or, in a few cases, who heard the stories from those who did. Once again, we're not talking about magic. It is not unusual for someone to pray or make a novena to Saint Anthony or Saint Jude and not get what he or she wants. I dare say that countless people with terminal illnesses prayed to Saint Jude and still died. No doubt an equally countless number of people prayed to Saint Anthony to find something they lost, and whatever it was stayed lost. All the same, I doubt that any of these people would say that their prayers were a waste of time.

In *Healing Words: The Power of Prayer and the Practice of Medicine*, Larry Dossey, M.D., discusses the scientific evidence for prayer as a method of physical healing. Dr. Dossey acknowledges that prayer does not bring about healing in every case. But, he says, scientific studies show that prayer does make a statistically significant difference, and it makes a difference often enough that it makes good sense to include prayer in a program of medical treatment.

The same is true when we lose something, or when we face what looks like an impossible situation. We should look high and low for what is lost, but it also makes sense to say a prayer, or make a novena, to Saint Anthony. When a hopeless situation arises, we should follow the doctor's advice and take our medication. But there is wisdom in asking Saint Jude to pray for us, too. We should pray to Saint Anthony or Saint Jude with persistence, because regardless of what else may or may not result, our prayers help us to be more aware of how close God is to us in our situation.

Dr. Dossey considers the question, If prayer makes a difference some of the time, why doesn't it make a difference all of the time? Think about it, he responds. If prayer brought about healing in all cases, the world would be overpopulated in no time because no one would die. Indeed, there would be no death. Christians believe that life does not find its ultimate fulfillment in this world, therefore it would not be good if prayer were to constitute a surefire method to cure all of the people all of the time.

Suffering and loss help us to grow up. If we could avoid

all suffering and loss by prayer to Saint Anthony or Saint Jude, we would remain emotionally and spiritually immature. Faith grows and deepens when we must cope with difficulty and darkness. Of course, getting what we pray for can nourish our faith, as well. Maybe that's why miracles and wonders continue to happen from time to time. Maybe miracles and wonders are like candy, however—too much would not be good for us.

Reading some of the stories here, you may find yourself thinking something like this: "Phooey. That result would have happened even if the person did not pray to Saint Anthony or Saint Jude."

My response would be, "Maybe yes, maybe no." Regardless, the person tells a true story about how he or she incorporated faith into an ordinary human situation. Perhaps the outcome would have been different if prayer had not been a part of the story, perhaps not. Who can say for sure after the fact? The point is that prayer is basic to the story. This is what happened, not something else. If you want to tell stories about lost things found with no appeal to Saint Anthony, or amazing events where prayer to Saint Jude played no part, go right ahead.

God Cares About the Small Stuff

Much skepticism about prayer is rooted in the presupposition—which can be neither proven nor disproven—that God has a singular disinterest in the piddling details of our everyday lives. Why should God give a tinker's damn whether I lost my paycheck, wedding ring, or car keys? The Creator of the universe has more important concerns than the illness of someone living in a small town in Nebraska. So goes this line of thought. But I think one of the main lessons of devotion to Saint Anthony or Saint Jude is that God is, indeed, interested in the small stuff, the ordinary sorrows and joys that fill our daily lives. Our God's merciful awareness is big enough to encompass even the small stuff, and two of God's "helpers" are Anthony and Jude, who lived human lives filled with details, as any human life is bound to be.

Christian faith is most authentic when we incorporate it into the fabric of our ordinary lives in the everyday world. To the extent that we limit our faith to certain times, places, and situations, we keep faith from having an impact on our life as a whole. To the extent that we allow faith to determine our lifestyle in every respect, to that extent our life will blossom and bear fruit. Devotion to Saint Anthony and/or Saint Jude is a way to incorporate faith into the most mundane, ordinary concerns of daily life. Is something lost? Faith belongs here, too, and there is a special friend of God you can talk to about it. His name is Anthony. A situation seems hopeless? Faith has a role to play, and God has another friend who's interested. His name is Jude. Pray to him. Maybe it's consistent with the will and wisdom of God to get what you pray for, maybe not. Either way, prayer does a body—and soul—good.

Devotion to Saint Anthony and Saint Jude endures, even in the face of disdain from theologians, professional liturgists, and ordinary Christians too sophisticated or too skeptical to pray to saints. Such people "think that relating to the sacred is awesome and unreachable except through the official teachings of the Church," or, I would add, through the writings of the latest religious guru, or the latest psycho-spiritual gimmick. This is what Dr. Robert Orsi, a professor of religious studies at Indiana University, told the *New York Times*. "But lots of people find access to what they consider the holy through the saints."

Introducing Saint Anthony

Anthony of Padua was born in 1195 in Lisbon, Portugal, and his baptismal name was Fernando. The son of Martin and Mary Bulhom—his father was a knight of the court of King Alfonso II—as a youth he studied under the priests of the cathedral in Lisbon. At the age of fifteen, he joined the Augustinian Order, which had a community near Lisbon. Two years later, he transferred to the same religious order's community at Coimbra. He was ordained a priest in 1219 or 1220—the records are unclear on this point.

In 1221, after he saw the bodies of the first Franciscan martyrs as they were carried through the town where he was living, Fernando decided to join the Franciscan Order and took the name Anthony. He went to Morocco to preach the gospel to the Moors, but he was forced by an illness to return to Italy, where he lived in a small hermitage, giving most of his time to prayer, reading the Scriptures, and doing menial work.

The same year, Anthony attended a general chapter, or meeting, of the Franciscan Order at Assisi, Italy. He was sent to the hospice of San Paoli, near Forli, and at an ordination there it turned out that no one had prepared a sermon. Oops. Anthony modestly volunteered and gave a spontaneous sermon that sparked his career as a famous preacher. After that, he was assigned to preach throughout Italy and became a spectacular success, what we today would call a celebrity. His sermons were so impressive that Anthony attracted huge crowds wherever he preached.

Because he was recognized as a man of deep prayer and an accomplished Bible and theology scholar, Anthony was named the first lector in theology for the Franciscans. He also became a minister provincial of his order and was named envoy from the 1226 general chapter to Pope Gregory IX. Seeing an opening, Anthony obtained the pope's release from his official duties to dedicate himself to preaching, and his success at winning converts to the faith was mind-boggling. He settled in Padua in 1226, where he attacked political corruption and completely reformed the city. Anthony worked on behalf of the poor, abolished debtors' prisons, and gave all his heart to trying to win people with weird ideas back to the faith. He was so effective that he won the nickname "Hammer of the Heretics."

In 1231, weary to the bone and sick with heart disease, Anthony traveled to Camposanpiero for a brief rest in 1231. On June 13, on the way back to Padua, he died of congestive heart failure, in a Poor Clare convent in Arcella, just outside Padua.

Franciscan scholar Sophronius Clasen, in *St. Anthony: Doctor of the Church*, says that immediately after Anthony's death

> Anthony became the object of an extraordinary devotion; and miracle followed miracle, as the prayers of the sick and afflicted were answered by sudden cures and other wonders. This set on foot a great wave of enthusiasm, and drew large crowds to his tomb, who began to honor him as a Saint even before the Pope canonized him. Often orderly processions were formed; and these were led sometimes by the bishop of Padua and his clergy. The leading knights of the city and the students of the university all took part; and all carried candles of great size.

Anthony was canonized a saint the year after his death, and in 1946 Pope Pius XII named him a Doctor of the Church. He is also known as "Wonder Worker."

Saint Anthony is the patron of the poor and oppressed, and alms given for his intercession are called "Saint Anthony's bread." Sometimes Anthony is pictured in religious art holding the infant Jesus. This depiction originated with one of Anthony's visitors during his lifetime who reported seeing this actually happen. Saint Anthony has more cities and places named for him than any other saint, write Franciscans Leonard Foley and Norman Perry, in *St. Anthony of Padua: The Story of His Life and Popular Devotions.* There are sixty-eight in all, including forty-four in Latin America, fifteen in the United States, four in Canada, four in the Philippines, and one in Spain. Four capes, three bays, two reefs, and two peaks are also named for him.

It is uncertain how Anthony became the saint to turn to when something is lost, but there is a story to go with the tradition. It seems that Anthony had a book of psalms that he treasured. Not only was any book valuable before the invention of the printing press, but Anthony kept in this book the notes he used to teach Franciscan students. A young man who grew weary of Franciscan life left the order and snatched Anthony's book on the way out. When Anthony realized his book was missing, he prayed that it would be found, and after this prayer the thief's heart was touched. He not only returned Anthony's book, but he took up again the life of a Franciscan friar, and the order accepted him back. The famous book of psalms is said to be on display in the Franciscan friary in Bologna, Italy.

Introducing Saint Jude

Saint Jude is sometimes called "Jude the Obscure," because we know so little about him. All the same, there is no doubt that he was an actual historical figure. Jude appears in the lists of the apostles of Jesus in the Gospel of Luke (6:16) and the Acts of the Apostles (1:13), where he is called "Judas [in other translations, 'Jude'] son of James," to distinguish him from Judas Iscariot, who betrayed Jesus. In the Gospels of Matthew (10:3) and Mark (3:18), he is called Thaddaeus or, in other translations, Thaddeus. Thus, sometimes Jude is called "Saint Jude Thaddeus."

A brief document in the New Testament, the Letter of Jude, bears the saint's name, but modern Scripture scholars seriously doubt that the Jude/Judas/Thaddaeus/Thaddeus named in the Gospels is the actual author of this document. The letter speaks of "the apostles of our Lord Jesus Christ" (1:17) as if they are figures of the distant past. Also, the excellent Greek in the letter is not likely to come from a Jewish follower of Jesus with little or no formal education. Finally, it was common for the later Christian community to give authority to a document or teaching by attributing it to an apostle or other early Christian teacher.

Devotion to Saint Jude originated rather recently and in the United States. In 1929, Father James Tort, a member of the Claretian Order, founded a shrine in honor of Saint Jude, in Chicago, Illinois. This shrine attracted people struggling with the terrible difficulties of the Great Depression. It was common at the time, said Dr. Robert Orsi, to finance church buildings through devotions to a particular saint. Devotions to Saint Jude, in Chicago, helped to pay off a church debt and helped to finance a seminary. Also, Dr. Orsi said, "Jude is attractive because he is not an ethnic saint. Jude is really an Americanized saint."

Saint Jude's association with hopeless situations is difficult to trace. It may come, at least in part, from the very obscurity that characterized the saint for centuries. Perhaps Jude's "guilt by association" with the betrayer of Christ led people to feel comfortable about telling him about their most hopeless problems. Jude had to put up with having the same name as Judas Iscariot, they reason, so he would understand the burden I'm dealing with, too. Perhaps Christians simply discovered a quality in Saint Jude—an interest in "hopeless cases"—and they respond to that quality in him.

Regardless of how devotion to Saint Jude started, the fact

remains that many, many people attend community novenas and other devotions to him at churches such as St. Francis of Assisi and St. Catherine of Siena in New York City. Of course, the original Shrine of Saint Jude in Chicago continues to attract many as well. As the stories in this book attest, even more people consider Saint Jude to be their personal friend.

The best-known story about Saint Jude, and one which increased the saint's popularity immensely, came from the late entertainer, Danny Thomas. In his autobiography *Make Room for Danny*, Danny Thomas explained that his faith had a lot to do with his success. The future celebrity, who then went by his actual name, Amos Jacobs, was so down-and-out in Detroit in the early years of his career that his wife wanted him to give up show business and become a grocery clerk. Then he heard about Saint Jude, the patron saint of hopeless situations. "When I first prayed to Saint Jude on that dark day in the Great Depression when my wife was expecting our first child, Marlo, I asked him to show me my way in life, and I vowed to build him a shrine. Soon after that, I had my first big success at the 5100 Club in Chicago, and I set out to fulfill my vow."

Attributing his success to the prayers of Saint Jude, Danny Thomas founded the world-famous St. Jude Children's Research Hospital in Memphis, Tennessee.

A Final Word

This book is about the recovery of an element of Christian piety—from the Latin, *pietas*, dutiful conduct—religious people today sometimes overlook or scoff at. This is even true among many who adhere to the Christian traditions— Roman Catholics, Orthodox believers, and Anglicans—that maintained a belief in the veneration of saints when Protestant traditions abandoned it. This book is about recovering a wider sense of the community of faith, one which includes the communion of saints. This book is about involvement with a dimension of Christian culture without which the Christian community is much the poorer.

According to the New Testament's Letter of James, Abraham "was called the friend of God" (2:23). To say that someone is a saint is to say that he or she is "the friend of God" in much the same way as Abraham. Anthony and Jude are friends of God, and because they are friends of God they are friends of God's people, as well. The stories that follow attest that Anthony and Jude can be good friends, indeed, to those open to their friendship.

Gather 'round and listen, not only with your ears but with your heart.

Part I

SAINT ANTHONY
OF PADUA

*Patron Saint
of Lost and Found*

How Can We Pay the Dentist?

In the depths of the Great Depression of the 1930s, Esther C. of Amherst, Wisconsin, lived on a farm in central Wisconsin with her parents, three brothers, and seven sisters. "We were a large family and though we always had plenty to eat on the farm," she recalled, "we had very little money."

Esther's older sister, Helen, lived in Milwaukee where she had a job, and she sent money home to her family from time to time.

Esther, then fifteen, and a younger sister, Stella, who was twelve, needed some dental work, but they had no money to pay the dentist. On a visit home, Helen gave her sisters fifteen dollars—a considerable sum in those days—so they could pay the dental bill.

On a freezing winter day, Esther and Stella set out to walk the three miles to the dentist's office in Wausau. "The roads were not plowed in those days," Esther said, "no one drove a car in the winter. The road was traveled by teams of horses and people on foot."

The icy air nipping at their noses, the two girls trudged through the snow, finally arriving at the dentist's office. After the girls' dental work was complete, Esther opened her purse to get the hard-earned money her older sister had given her. The money was gone.

"It was very embarrassing," Esther said. She explained to the dentist that the money was missing, and he was very irritated, thinking the girls were trying to cheat him. Esther and Stella decided that Esther must have left the money at home on her dresser. Back into the cold and snow the girls went, hoping they were right about the money being still at home. Soon, they met a neighbor who also happened to be in Wausau. They told him their story, and he kindly loaned the girls the money to pay the dentist.

When Esther and Stella arrived home, they immediately looked on Esther's dresser for the money, but it was not there. By this time it was already growing dark. Still, Helen urged the girls to go back outside and look for the money. Perhaps Esther had dropped it by accident along the way. Esther then remembered opening her purse to get a hanky as they walked along earlier that day, about a mile from home.

Esther and Stella said a prayer to Saint Anthony, asking him to pray that they might find the lost money. As they walked along, their noses and cheeks freezing, and darkness almost upon them, they nearly gave up hope. On the verge of turning back, suddenly the girls saw a five- and a ten-dollar bill lying on the snow. "They had laid there all afternoon in plain sight," Esther recalled, "in plain sight of anyone who passed by. We knew then that Saint Anthony covered them for us as any traveler could have easily seen them and picked them up."

"Please Help Me Find My Parakeet"

Maryanne M. of Woodbury, New Jersey, recalls a "Saint Anthony experience" from 1981: "I was still in high school and working part time at a fast-food restaurant. I got home from work late one night to find my parakeet had escaped from his cage." Maryanne searched all throughout the house but couldn't find the bird anywhere. "So I prayed," said Maryanne. "[I said,] 'Saint Anthony, I'm sure you have more important things to do, but please help me find my parakeet.' (I was afraid my cat would get her.)"

Maryanne continued her search into the foyer. "My mom had a votive candle, a statue of the Blessed Mother, and some pictures on the wall," said Maryanne, describing the room. "Guess who was sitting perched on Saint Anthony's picture? Yup—my parakeet. A coincidence maybe, but I believe he helped me find her."

An Heirloom Rosary Is Lost

In the early 1970s, Genevieve J. of Columbia, New Jersey, inherited a very old rosary—which came originally from Europe—when her mother-in-law died. Not only was the rosary easy to identify because it was so old, but attached to the crucifix was a medal with an image of Saint Francis of Assisi on one side, "and on the other side," Genevieve said, "a rather fat Saint Anthony (spelled Antony) with the child Jesus."

Twenty years later, in the fall of 1992, Genevieve drove the fourteen miles from her home in rural New Jersey to a supermarket. Her shopping completed, she pushed her cart to the checkout counter. While searching her pockets for small change, she took out her house keys and her heirloom rosary and set them on the counter. She paid her bill, then left the store.

Only when she arrived home did Genevieve remember that she had left her house keys and rosary at the supermarket checkout counter. "But I wasn't about to go back fourteen miles," she said. Instead, Genevieve prayed to Saint Anthony, asking him to keep her rosary and keys safe until she made another trip into town.

A week later, Genevieve returned to the supermarket and asked if her keys and rosary had been found. The keys were safe, but the rosary was missing. Sad, but resigned to the loss of her rosary, Genevieve prayed, asking Saint Anthony that whoever had her beads might use them with respect. But this was not to be the end of the story.

One day in May 1993, Genevieve went to the beauty salon near her home for her regular appointment to have her hair done. To her astonishment, hanging on a nail on the wall above the cashier's desk was a rosary that looked familiar. Genevieve asked the young woman at the desk where the rosary came from.

Genevieve learned that for the past six months a lady had come to have her hair done every week, and while she sat under the hair dryer she prayed using the rosary that now hung on the wall. The last time she came to the salon she left the rosary hanging on the arm of the chair she had been seated in while her hair dried.

A few weeks later, the woman's husband came into the salon and told the women who worked there that his wife had died, a victim of cancer, the week before. The woman offered him the rosary beads, but he said, "No." The rosary had hung on the wall of the beauty salon since that day.

Genevieve asked to examine the rosary more closely, and to her amazement there was no question that this was the old rosary she inherited from her mother-in-law. "Fourteen miles and six months later, there were my beads."

With a Little Help From a (Canine) Friend

Since she was twelve years old, Marie S. of Cherry Hill, New Jersey, wore around her neck a blue Miraculous Medal, a small medallion imprinted with an image of Mary, the mother of Jesus. This medal reflects a devotion related to three apparitions of Mary to Catherine Labourè in France in 1830. Marie received her Miraculous Medal from a very dear cousin. "Upon receiving the medal," Marie said, "I decided to wear it always as a link between us."

As the years passed, Marie lost her medal many times when the light chain around her neck, upon which the medal was suspended, would break. Each time, she prayed to Saint Anthony, asking him to help her find the medal, and always the medal turned up.

In the late 1970s, however, Marie lost her medal and thought that maybe this time it was gone for good. "I missed the medal from my chain," she said, "and prayed very hard to Saint Anthony to help me."

The medal was missing for several weeks, and Marie gave up hope of ever finding it again. At that time, Marie and her husband had a large black and white dog named Grunner. The friendly dog was Marie's constant companion. One day, Grunner started to behave in an unusual fashion. He sat by the door to a pantry closet in Marie's kitchen, something he had never done before. There was nothing in the closet of any interest to Grunner, nothing to eat, nothing to get playful with.

Grunner pawed at the closet door. Curious, Marie opened the door. On the floor of the pantry closet she kept used paper and plastic bags from the supermarket for future use. Grunner began to pull the bags out with his forepaws, and when Marie tried to stop him from scattering the bags, he would not be stopped.

Marie decided there must be something behind the bags that Grunner wanted, so she removed the bags herself. To her amazement, lying in the corner of the pantry closet was her tiny blue medal. "Saint Anthony had used old Grunner as an instrument in helping me find my precious medal."

Mom Had an "In" With Saint Anthony

Marge F. of Shrewsbury, Missouri, said that her mother had an "in" with Saint Anthony, something her family took for granted. One day Marge's mother was "very agitated" because she couldn't locate her rosary. Marge asked, "Mom, did you pray to Saint Anthony?" With exasperation in her voice, she replied, "Of course I prayed to Saint Anthony!"

A minute later, Marge's mother stood in the middle of the room, no furniture or lamps anywhere nearby. As she stood puzzling over where her rosary might be, the lost rosary dropped on the floor in front of her.

Another time, one winter day Marge was walking home using a route so familiar to her that she never gave her surroundings a second glance. Some possibly treacherous ice near a driveway caught Marge's eye, and she happened to look down. There lay a cameo brooch with an image of Mary, the mother of Jesus, on it, a brooch Marge knew belonged to her mother.

As she stepped into the house, Marge asked her mother if she was missing anything. "No," she replied. Marge said, "Mom, Saint Anthony isn't even waiting for you to pray anymore. Here is your brooch!"

Find That Baseball!

Craig G. of Duquesne, Pennsylvania, said that as a young boy, his mother always reminded him to say a prayer to Saint Anthony whenever he misplaced a shirt or toy. "The prayer would calm me and give me a clearer head, and I would remember where I put my lost toy or shirt," he said.

When Craig got older, he developed a love for baseball. Often, the "pickup" games were interrupted when a batter hit the ball over the hillside into "tall weeds." Craig would automatically pray to Saint Anthony to find the wayward ball. "As I would finish my prayer," Craig said, "and be relaxed, I then would proceed over to the area where I thought the ball would be, and I yelled 'I found it!' many, many a time."

As an adult, Craig's love for baseball endured, and he even had his own semipro baseball team. Craig was an owner/manager/player, and he still chased foul balls. "I knew I could find the baseballs when others would give up," he said. "I knew that Saint Anthony was with me; I felt it. And with this confidence I very rarely lost a baseball."

Craig said that the beauty of Saint Anthony was that as an eight-year-old boy he learned to carry the Spirit with him as he looked for a lost baseball, and he was doing the same when he was forty years old.

"As I prayed to Saint Anthony in search of a baseball, I drew closer to God, being ever so thankful for the blessing of playing baseball, a game I loved, all the while thanking God for the gift of doing so."

Finding Lost Words

Dorothy M. of Sarasota, Florida, at age eighty-four sometimes found it difficult to remember words and names. "They are not at hand when I want to say them," she explained. "I know they are somewhere in my mind; so I just pray to Saint Anthony, and sure enough he always gives the word I'm searching for—sometimes immediately, sometimes later, even days or weeks later."

Once Dorothy wanted to send a new belt to her granddaughter, but the only word she could think of was "girdle." When she used "girdle" to explain what she wanted to send, she knew that must have mystified her granddaughter. "She probably doesn't even know what a girdle is!"

Another time, Dorothy wanted to say "staircase," but the only word she could think of was "veranda." She couldn't recall the word "monstrance"—an ornate implement sometimes used in Catholic churches to display the consecrated eucharistic bread, for special eucharistic devotions. All Dorothy could think of was "that thing with all the gold rays coming out that they show the host in."

In each case, after praying to Saint Anthony to help her find the lost words, Dorothy found the word she was looking for.

"Where Are Your Coats?"

It was Easter Sunday 1936. Five-year-old Dorothy M., now of Blackwood, New Jersey, and her sister, Eleanor, age four, played outside their home on a small street in southwest

Philadelphia, Pennsylvania. They wore their new Easter dresses, topped with matching coats—pink for Dorothy, blue for Eleanor.

The girls' mother called, "Time to come in." When Dorothy and Eleanor got into the house, their mother asked, "Where are your coats?" The little girls looked at each other, then remembered that they had gotten warm while playing. They had taken off their coats, but they could not remember where they had put them. "Losing brand new coats in days when money was not very plentiful," Dorothy said, "was tantamount to a catastrophe."

The girls and their parents went outside to look for the coats. They covered the little street—no parked cars in those days—from one end to the other, including the alley three houses away. No luck. Neighbors joined in the search, but nobody found the coats.

"I remember my mother saying, 'Well, we'll say a prayer to Saint Anthony. There's nothing more we can do now as it's getting dark.'"

Some time later, the girls' mother stepped out on the porch of their home. "Silhouetted by a golden glow from the gas light a short distance from the house hung the two little coats on the lamppost!" Dorothy said.

The Film I Took of the Pope Is Missing!

When Pope John Paul II visited Denver, Colorado, in the summer of 1993, Donna F. of Upper Darby, Pennsylvania, was a delegate to the International Youth Forum that preceded World Youth Day. Donna was fortunate enough to meet John Paul II.

Donna exposed five rolls of film taking pictures of the pope and other people she met in Denver, but when she mailed the rolls of film for processing they disappeared for more than a month. Donna did not have the film, and neither did the photo-processing company.

"Pete, a good friend at work, said to pray to Saint Anthony," Donna explained. "I thought he was joking. But he said, 'I will pray to him for you.' "

Soon, one by one the rolls of film arrived at Donna's home by mail, fully developed into beautiful photographs. She thanked Pete, but he said, "Don't thank me, thank Saint Anthony; he never lets you down."

You Have Twenty Minutes, Saint Anthony!

Sister Barbara K., director of a family ministry office in Saint Cloud, Minnesota, professed a great dependence upon Saint Anthony. "For many years," she said, "I have relied upon Saint Anthony and have a special relationship with him. Whenever I have misplaced something or forgotten something, I make my request and usually let Saint Anthony know that I need whatever has been lost in a certain amount of time. I then go about my business and leave it in his capable hands."

One time, Sister Barbara needed some papers with some important statistics on them for a meeting. She knew she had filed the papers, but where? The meeting would begin in half an hour. What could she do?

"Look," Sister Barbara prayed to Saint Anthony, "I have twenty minutes to find those papers. Could you please help me find them?" She then turned her attention to something else entirely. When the twenty minutes were up, Sister Barbara returned to the file cabinet she had been searching frantically a few minutes before, and the first thing she saw was the file folder she needed.

A Stolen Bicycle

Mrs. William S. of Lewes, Delaware, received the news one day that her grandson's bicycle had been stolen from the front porch of his family's home. The theft was reported to the police, but Mrs. S. believed Saint Anthony could help. So many bicycles are stolen each year, it seemed unlikely that her grandson's bike would turn up. Mrs. S. prayed daily asking Saint Anthony to help recover her grandson's bike...and after two months the bicycle was found.

"After such a long time, we consider that a miracle," Mrs. S. said.

"I Yelled at Saint Anthony"

Six days went by, and Monica D. of Bay Shore, New York, still could not find her lost hearing aid. "I turned the house upside down looking for it," she said. She also prayed several times each day asking Saint Anthony to help her find the lost hearing aid.

On the sixth day, Monica arrived home from work and collected the mail from her mailbox. Among the bills and junk mail was a letter from a Franciscan missionary organization together with a card with Saint Anthony's picture on it.

"I sort of slammed the picture down on the dining-room table and said, 'You know, Saint Anthony, I have been praying to you for six days and I am getting nowhere. Will you please tell me where that hearing aid is? I can't afford to put out five hundred dollars for a new one!' "

Monica wondered how Saint Anthony could tell her where her hearing aid was, especially since she had looked everywhere two or three times. She decided to open her Bible at random—an idea which made her laugh, as if the Bible could tell her to look under the television set or behind the VCR. All the same, Monica flipped open her Bible, and the place it fell open at was Psalm 6. She read verse 6: "I am weary with my moaning...." That described her, all right. She read on. "...I flood my bed with tears; I drench my couch with my weeping."

Into her bedroom Monica went, to check the bed for the umpteenth time. No hearing aid. Then she took the pillows off her couch—for at least the third time—and…there was the hearing aid!

"Truthfully," Monica said, "I yelled so loud at Saint Anthony maybe he figured he had better tell me where my hearing aid was. I think he waited so long to teach me a lesson about being so careless."

Dad Said to Pray to Saint Anthony

Norene P. of Verdigre, Nebraska, treasures the memory of a day in February 1980 when her fifth child, Sarah, received "a lovely white banded watch" for her eighth birthday, a gift chosen by her father. A few evenings later, Sarah was being her usual lively eight-year-old self, practicing her tumbling in the living room. She thought she had taken off her new wrist watch and put it on the coffee table, but when she went to get the watch it was gone.

With her parents' help, Sarah searched the house for her watch, but no luck. Finally, Sarah's father, "in his usual quiet, gentle manner," suggested that Sarah pray to Saint Anthony. He was sure Saint Anthony would help them to find the lost watch.

"So," Norene said, "Sarah and I went to the bathroom and took from the wall the little copper plaque of Saint Anthony, the one her husband had kept from his boyhood home. Together, Norene and her daughter read the prayer to Saint Anthony from the back of the plaque. Then they went to Sarah's bedroom, and Sarah knelt by her bed to say her usual bedtime prayers with another petition to Saint Anthony added for good measure.

Just then, Sarah's father quietly entered the bedroom and asked Sarah if she had said her prayers to Saint Anthony. Sarah said that she had. Then she saw that in her father's hand was her lost watch with the white wrist band. Her father had gone to his desk in the basement and there was the watch.

Sarah could not remember having been in the basement, although she had, in fact, visited her mother there after school that day. But there seemed no reason for her to have taken off her watch at that time. Sarah said that it was certainly lucky that her father happened to go down to this desk to get something, otherwise her watch would not have been found that night.

"She was one happy little child," Norene said. "Bless Saint Anthony."

"All Our Money Was in That Purse!"

When she was a newlywed, Patricia R. of Wichita, Kansas, traveled with her husband and her brother and sister to the resort town of Colorado Springs, Colorado. The town was teeming with tourists, and every place seemed to be crowded. Patricia's little group went into a cafe to eat lunch one day, and then they went back to the hotel where they were staying. There Patricia realized that she did not have her purse. "This was a disaster," she said, "because all our money was in that purse, and we didn't have much."

The little group of travelers rushed back to the cafe where they had eaten, but the purse was gone and had not been turned in at the cashier's desk. Now what?

"My husband was a great believer in the prayers of Saint Anthony," Patricia said. "We all prayed hard and decided to go from shop to shop in the hope that we would find the purse."

Finally, after visiting many shops and stores, Patricia and her companions entered a cafe where some women were seated at a booth. Patricia saw that one of the women had two purses, and one of them was Patricia's. "I walked over to her, took the purse and said, 'This is my purse.' The woman did not say a word or reach for the purse, she just watched us walk away."

How could this happen in a town crowded with people, Patricia wondered, without the help of Saint Anthony?

Saint Anthony's Dream

"When I was a little girl," reported Patricia R. of Wichita, Kansas, "I used my dad's pen without permission and then couldn't remember what I had done with it."

Before she went to bed, Patricia prayed to Saint Anthony to help her find her father's pen before he discovered it was missing. That night, she dreamed that the pen was in a certain drawer of her father's desk.

The next morning, Patricia ran to see if her dream was correct, and sure enough it was. "The pen was there just as I had dreamed."

A Small Miracle

Where could the paycheck be? Diane D. of Miami, Florida, knew that her husband's paycheck had to be someplace, but somehow it had gotten lost. "I'll pray to Saint Anthony," she thought. Her husband's union was about to go on strike, and this was the last check the family would receive for who knew how many weeks.

Diane decided to begin a novena to Saint Anthony, asking him to help find the missing paycheck. "My baby," she said, "who was just creeping, pulled a box from the trash to be burned, opened it, and the paycheck fell at my feet, just as I completed the first prayer of the novena."

Diane said the rest of her novena to Saint Anthony in thanksgiving.

A Ten-Dollar Bill Takes Flight

In the early 1950s, Mrs. W. of Corvallis, Oregon, was awakened by her mother telling her that she had been working in her flower garden. A ten-dollar bill Mrs. W.'s mother had in her pocket had gotten lost while she was weeding her flowers.

An imaginative woman, Mrs. W.'s mother cut pieces of paper the size of her missing ten-spot, then she went to where she had been when she realized her money was gone, and she let the wind carry the pieces of paper to see where they would go. This creative tactic had no results, however, and now here she was in her daughter's bedroom asking her to say a prayer to Saint Anthony to help her find her ten-dollar bill.

"After searching for some time," Mrs. W. said, "I became suspicious that my mother did not have the faith in Saint Anthony that I had, so I asked her if she thought we'd find the bill. She said she didn't and that we might as well give up. I said, 'Not me—but I want you to go, as Saint Anthony will not work for you if you do not believe.' "

Mrs. W.'s mother smiled and left. The moment she was out of sight, the girl saw the ten-dollar bill on the toe of her shoe. The mother always thought her daughter had replaced the missing bill with one of her own. "I knew better!" Mrs. W. said.

"Please Find My Brother!"

Together with her elderly parents, Catherine O. of Charleston, South Carolina, visited Ireland to renew old family ties. One day, they visited the cemetery where Catherine's Uncle Michael—her mother's brother—was buried next to his parents. Catherine and her parents marveled at the astonishing series of events that brought Michael to his final resting place in Ireland.

Michael was born in Ireland in 1888 and joined the Christian Brothers, a Catholic religious order dedicated to teaching, at the age of eighteen. A few years later, Michael was sent to the Christian Brothers' college in Hong Kong to teach English.

Years passed, Michael never wrote home, and when his parents inquired they learned that he had left the Christian Brothers and his whereabouts were unknown. While still at the college in Hong Kong, Michael's sister—Catherine's mother—wrote to him from her home in Philadelphia, Pennsylvania. Michael never replied, but he did keep the letter with his sister's address.

For over fifty years, Catherine's mother prayed to Saint Anthony to find her brother, Michael, or at least to turn up some word of what had happened to him. She often said that he was a very gentle, kind, and handsome young man, and she loved him very much.

In 1962, a letter arrived from the Philippine Islands from two teachers who had come across Michael living near them. They had found the letter Catherine's mother had written to Michael so many years before and thought she would want to know that he was a very sick, senile old man living in poverty. The teachers wrote that Michael had once been very successful dealing in mahogany, but he lost his business, as well as his wife and children, when the Japanese invaded the Philippines during World War II. They added that Michael would never speak about the loss of his family, looking on the past as a bad dream.

Immediately, Catherine's mother contacted the Catholic bishop near where Michael lived, and with the bishop's help Michael traveled by airplane to Philadelphia. "He arrived in terrible physical condition at the age of seventy-three," Catherine said.

After a two-month stay in the hospital, Michael insisted that he wanted to return to Ireland where another sister still lived on the old family homestead. He lived in Ireland with his sister for two years and died of a stroke at age seventy-five. Michael was waked in the parish church where he had been baptized and buried beside his parents and two brothers.

"Saint Anthony had indeed performed another miracle," Catherine said, "and my mother's prayers to him for over fifty years had truly been answered."

"Tony, Tony, Look Around!"

Patrick, the third of Faith M.'s five children, was born on Saint Anthony's Day, June 13, in 1963. "From an early age," she said, "he understood his role as the family's chief mediator with the saint, and he learned the prayer, 'Tony, Tony, look around. Something's lost and must be found.' Actually, since our need was more often finding the *un*found rather than the *lost*, we most often recited this version: 'Tony, Tony, look around. Something hasn't yet been found.' "

Faith, who lives in New York City, recalled that on many family trips when they needed to get to a train on time or find a taxi when none was in sight, Patrick got busy with the prayer to Saint Anthony and, "sure enough, a cab would somehow materialize. Saint Anthony always provided."

On a bitterly cold November night in 1973, Patrick put Saint Anthony to the acid test. "It had been a mild evening," Faith recalled, "when I took Patrick on the bus to Lincoln Center. He was a member of the New York City Opera Children's Chorus, and would be in *Faust* that night."

After dropping Patrick off at the New York State Theater's stage entrance, Faith went off to visit a friend who was in the hospital. Since the children's chorus was in the first and final acts, she knew she would have plenty of time before it would be time to retrieve Patrick from the theater. At the same time, Faith knew it would be a hassle to get Patrick home because by the time the kids took off their costumes and scrubbed off their makeup the audience would have a head start getting cabs.

"What I *didn't* know," Faith said, "was that within just a few hours the temperature would plunge alarmingly, and that it was one of those Worst Scenario nights when *all* the Lincoln Center performances ended at *the same time.*"

This meant that Patrick and Faith, clad only in thin jackets because the weather had been so mild earlier in the evening, would have to compete with thousands of public transportation-seekers from not just City Opera but also from the Met and the Philharmonic.

Faith met her son as he emerged from backstage, and as soon as the two were outside Faith knew they were in trouble. "If *Faust* had brought to mind the Fires of Hell," she said, "the image was quickly dispelled by bone-chilling icy blasts."

As Patrick and Faith shivered their way across the plaza, they could see that already there were long lines at the bus stops and large crowds competed fiercely whenever a taxi appeared. "Clearly this was a crisis situation."

Mother and son decided to split up. She would join the crowd hoping to board a bus on 62nd Street, he would elbow his way through the cab-seeking crowd. "We would keep an eye on each other and would take whichever came first—if anything ever did."

Mother and son kept saying, through chattering teeth, their Saint Anthony prayer: "Tony [shiver, shiver], Tony, look around. Something hasn't yet been found."

Faith didn't see it coming, but suddenly there it was—a taxi screeched to a stop right in front of Patrick. "Now this might not seem so miraculous," Faith said. "After all, it was past eleven, here's this skinny kid in a flimsy jacket competing with all these big people. It could touch a cabby's heart." But guess what happened next.

Patrick and his mother gratefully climbed into the taxi. The cab driver looked around, gave them a big smile, and said: "Hi! My name's Tony."

Mike Royko Tells a Saint Anthony Story

Sometimes Saint Anthony shows up in the most remarkable places. Jane O. of Oak Lawn, Illinois, for example, shared a story about Saint Anthony written up by *Chicago Tribune* columnist Mike Royko.

"My grandmother was a strong believer in Saint Anthony's powers, and so I inherited that," Jane said. "Now my husband, family, and children all call on the good saint many times over, and he never fails. We always find what we've lost, even if it takes a bit of time. I'm sure he's very busy!"

In a column titled, "Miracle's Sad End Par for the Course," Mike Royko wrote: "Maybe you don't believe in miracles, faith or the power of prayer.

"These are not subjects I write about frequently. In fact, I don't think I ever have."

Royko went on to tell a story he found "so amazing that I must pass it on to those who have disdain for the spiritual life."

Anne B., principal of Our Lady of Lourdes School in Chicago, and Ginger D., a longtime teacher at the same school, enjoyed playing golf most Fridays after school, weather permitting. "They aren't very good," Royko quipped, "but 90 percent of all golfers aren't very good, so that doesn't matter."

Usually, Anne and Ginger played golf at a public course in Chicago's northwest suburbs. But on October 1, 1993, the two women decided to play at another course. (The plot thickens.)

Anne said, "Our usual Friday routine is, I correct the spelling tests, Ginger changes into her golf clothes, then I make the end-of-the-day announcements and by 2:35 we are in the car.

"That day, we were going to Rob Roy, our favorite course. But I said, 'Let's go to Skokie Playfields instead.'"

"That," Mike Royko explained, "is the village-owned golf course in wealthy Winnetka."

Anne wasn't sure why she decided to switch courses. "It's like we were drawn to that place."

"Before we teed off," Ginger said, "a golf attendant tells us some lady lost a diamond bracelet and is frantic, so we said, 'Oh, sure, no big deal.' So we started playing and we got to the second hole and a man in a suit drives up in a cart with a blond woman in the cart."

"She was beautiful," Anne said. "Probably in her late thirties. Blond hair pulled back in a French braid, thin, definitely a size six."

Ginger added, "Oh, she was the mold. Beautiful, natural blond, a great figure. Winnetka mother, dressed perfectly for golf. A beautiful woman. And her outfit...."

"It was just perfect," Anne said. "She was wearing beige shorts with a very expensive beige and white sweater, matching, of course, with coordinated shoes."

Mike Royko interjected: "If [the two women] sound a bit catty, keep in mind that Catholic school employees are not among the highest paid in the education field. Few wear cashmere."

"So," Ginger continued, "we're waiting at the second hole, and there's this beautiful woman in the cart. The man tells us about the lost bracelet. And I tell the woman: 'You should say a prayer to Saint Anthony.' And she said, 'I don't have time to deal with that. My husband is going to kill me.' So I said a prayer out loud anyway. I said: 'Dear Saint Anthony, we pray, bring it back without delay.'"

At that, the beautiful woman tooled away in her golf cart, while Anne and Ginger teed off. Ginger plopped her ball in an inconvenient creek.

"As we were looking in the water," Anne said, "which was real murky, I saw something sparkling. So I yelled, 'We found it, we found it!' And I put my hand in the muck—yuck!—and I pulled out this bracelet. And it was big."

"We're talking *big!*" Ginger said. "A row of diamonds on heavy gold in an intricate little pattern. Stunning. So we both yell and wave our arms to catch the golf cart with the woman."

Anne continued: "So she comes running over and puts her arms around me and gives me this big hug. She's hugging me and thanking me."

"But she didn't cry," Ginger added.

"Nope. Not a tear," Anne said. "Then she said she had to get my name and phone number. So I wrote it down for her. And we told her we worked for a Catholic school. And we told her that anything we got would go to the school. And we meant it."

"We were told by a man on the course," Ginger said, "that he heard the woman say it was worth thousands."

After the woman drove away in her golf cart, Ginger and Anne finished their round of golf. "Then," Mike Royko commented, "they began to wait."

"It was a week," Anne recalled. "Then two. Ginger kept asking if she called."

"Not even a note," Ginger said.

Anne said that she was "a little disappointed." After all, it isn't every day people find diamond bracelets and give them back.

"But our students think it is a cool story," Ginger said. "I think the title should be, 'Honesty is its own reward.' We use it to teach. Of course, we wouldn't mind if she felt really bad."

Mike Royko was skeptical at first. Then he called the golf pro at the course where this happened and asked about the two women's story. "Yeah, it happened here," the golf pro said. "It's a true, goofy story. She came in here and said she needed help finding it. I figured it was like a needle in a haystack.

"But they met those two people, and they said a prayer.

No sooner had they said it, they found it in some obscure place. It's weird."

Mike Royko said: "So ye of little faith, think about it. Especially when you are walking past a water hole.

"And ye rich blonds who lose bracelets on a golf course—come on, send them a check."

As of the writing of this book, no check had arrived at Our Lady of Lourdes School in Chicago from a certain wealthy blond woman. Anne said, however, that because of Royko's column, she and Ginger received many kind notes and even a few nice checks for the school.

A Mexican Adventure

Time: the early 1950s. Place: Mexico. Anna M. of Bloomington, Minnesota, drove south of the border with three friends on vacation. One of the three friends owned the car they traveled in and was the principal driver on the trip. "She had only one set of keys," Anna said, "and she entrusted them to no one else. If someone else drove, she pocketed the keys as soon as the motor was turned off."

One afternoon, the four friends visited an old convent that had been converted into a museum. This was during the era in Mexico's history when it was illegal for Catholic priests and members of religious orders to wear religious garb in public and live in community. The convent-museum sat in the middle of a large open field, and for an hour or more Anna and her friends wandered around, inside and out and around all four walls of the old building. "I don't remember seeing a single person anywhere around," Anna said.

The four women left the interesting old building and headed back to the car. The driver rummaged through her purse and exclaimed frantically that she could not find her keys. The other three women wrung their hands wondering what to do next. The driver cried and fumed, blaming her friends for staying so long. It would soon be dark, what were they to do? It seemed hopeless to find a set of keys in such a large field.

As she surveyed the field, spreading out in all directions, Anna began to pray asking Saint Anthony for help. "In only a matter of minutes, after I began praying," Anna remembered, "I walked right straight to the keys in the middle of this huge field, picked them up, and handed them to my friend who was driving."

Anna is a Catholic but her three friends were all Protestants, and they asked her how she managed to find the keys. "I didn't," she said. "It was Saint Anthony who led me directly to the keys."

None of Anna's three friends were convinced by her story about praying to Saint Anthony. "Yet," she said, "in the car I had the feeling they knew something like a little miracle had happened. I thanked Saint Anthony one more time."

In Your Face, Saint Anthony!

About a week after her mother's death, Sister Carol C. of Watervliet, New York, stopped by her father's apartment to see how he was doing. Sister Carol was startled to find her father "really agitated" because he had lost the ring his wife had given him the last Christmas before she suffered a stroke.

"He was frantically searching every corner of the apartment," Sister Carol said, "and, of course, I joined the cause."

After about twenty minutes of what Sister Carol called "fruitless sweeping, reaching, peeking, and poking," she said, "Dad, why don't we say a little prayer to Saint Anthony; he's never failed me, and I doubt he'd fail you."

Sister Carol's father was by now so frustrated he was pulling towels out of the linen closet and tossing them on the floor. "Come on, Saint Anthony, I don't have time for this," he muttered. "Where's the ring?"

At that moment, the ring came flying out between two towels Sister Carol's father had dragged from the closet. Apparently, when he had put the towels away the ring had slipped from his finger between the two towels.

"I don't think I've ever seen my dad so surprised," Sister Carol said. "You can be sure he really depends on Saint Anthony to this day."

All I Want From Saint Anthony
Is My One Front Tooth!

During World War II, Ann P.'s husband was wounded in combat. Sent to the Teddy Roosevelt Estate in Oyster Bay, New York, to recuperate, Ann went to visit him one Sunday. He was upset because he had lost his false front tooth while walking on the nearby rocky beach. "He had looked all over," said Ann, who now lives in Hungtington Station, New York, "and he could not find it among all those pebbles."

Ann suggested to her husband that he say a prayer to Saint Anthony and he would be sure to find his tooth. "I told him to promise Saint Anthony that he would go back to church."

"Oh, sure," Ann's husband said, laughing, "Saint Anthony's going to find my tooth among all those pebbles."

When Ann returned the following week she found her husband excited. He explained that he and a few other men had gone walking on the beach. He had said with a joking manner, "My wife thinks Saint Anthony is going to find my tooth."

Ann's husband stopped walking and with a bit of a mocking tone in his voice, pointed to the pebbles at his feet and said loudly, "Saint Anthony find my tooth!" He looked down and much to his astonishment there was his lost tooth.

A Love Letter (From Saint Anthony) in the Sand

In 1966, Eleanor C. of Ocean City, New Jersey, lived with her husband and children near Philadelphia. After three or four summer weeks stuck in the house with children who had mumps, Eleanor was elated when her husband suggested she take their daughter Jane—who did not have the mumps—and go to a nearby swimming pool for a couple of hours.

"Delightedly I packed our swimming gear," Eleanor recalled, "and Jane and I set forth for an afternoon of relaxation."

The pool Eleanor and her daughter went to had a beach surrounding it, and Eleanor was so eager to submerge herself in the cool water that she put her beach bag down on the sand and jumped into the pool without remembering to don her rubber bathing cap, which pool regulations required.

From the water, Eleanor called to Jane to toss her bathing cap so she could put it on. Jane plucked the bathing cap from her mother's beach bag and threw it to her mother.

After a refreshing swim, mother and daughter decided it was time to head for home—and that was when Eleanor discovered that her car keys were missing. Obviously, they were catapulted out of the bag when Jane threw the bathing cap to her mother. Eleanor began to search frantically for the keys. Lifeguards, pool attendants, and other swimmers joined the search for the lost keys. Someone brought rakes to comb the sand, but to no avail.

For eleven days the keys remained lost, but Eleanor and her family kept praying to Saint Anthony for the keys to be returned. After eleven days, however, they began to accept that the keys were lost for good. "We reckoned, however, without the help of Saint Anthony," Eleanor said, "because even though my faith in his intercession was beginning to waver, I continued to pray to him."

On the twelfth day, Eleanor and Jane returned to the pool. As they sat on the beach, Eleanor began to run her hand through the sand. To her great surprise and undying gratitude to Saint Anthony, her fingers wrapped around her lost keys.

"My Left Hand Felt Different"

"About ten years ago," recalls Rosalie V. of Dover, New Hampshire, "I was a very busy wife, mother of two teenagers, and part-time university student."

On one very busy day, Rosalie had attended a couple of classes at the university of New Hampshire, gone to the pool to swim laps, went grocery shopping, and returned home about 1:00 P.M. After lunch Rosalie went down to the basement to put in a load of clothes in the washing machine.

It was when she came back upstairs that Rosalie noticed something. "My left hand felt different. Without looking, I touched my engagement and wedding rings, and they felt strange. When I looked down at them, I saw this big, gaping hole where my almost one-carat diamond had rested for seventeen years."

Rosalie had been to so many places, she didn't know where or when it came out!

Rosalie tried not to panic as she began looking around the house for the diamond. "My worst fear," said Rosalie, "was that it had come off while loading the washing machine and was now merrily on its way to the sewer system!"

Rosalie was on her hands and knees searching the rug when her son came home from school. By this time Rosalie was in tears.

"My son suggested I call my husband at work. I said, 'What good will that do?' He said, 'Well, Dad will buy you another one.' I said that I didn't want 'another one'—I wanted *that* one!"

It was then that Rosalie remembered Anthony, the patron saint of lost articles. She said a brief prayer to Saint Anthony, asking his assistance in finding her diamond.

"About two hours had passed since I became aware of my loss," said Rosalie. "I went downstairs to put the washed clothes in the dryer and lo and behold!—there on the bottom stair, clear as day, was the diamond glinting up at me! And it was a dark stairway, too!"

After she had the diamond reset into the same setting, Rosalie gathered together her family for a special ceremony. A priest blessed the ring as Rosalie's husband placed it on her finger. "And there it has remained continually for the last ten years," stated Rosalie. "Thanks to Saint Anthony!"

"He Would Lose His Job for Sure"

Helen W. of Saint Petersburg, Florida, has a son named Roger who, she said, is no longer a churchgoing person. All the same, Saint Anthony responded to a prayer from her son.

As a traveling salesman, Roger spent much of his time in hotels. One day, Roger walked down the hallway in the hotel he was staying in at the time. He noticed a security guard looking anxiously around the floor Roger's room was on, and when he asked the man what the problem was he explained that he had lost the large bunch of keys to all the locks on that floor. If he didn't find them he would lose his job for sure.

"My son Roger," Helen said, "actually prayed to Saint Anthony for the poor man, just as his mother would do!"

Roger went to bed early that evening, and as he slid between the sheets he felt something hard at the foot of his bed. "It was the security man's bunch of keys!" Helen said, and they were in a most unusual place for a security guard's keys to be.

Roger hurried after the guard, and he was so overjoyed that he said again and again, "God bless you, young man!"

"I Lost My Dime for Milk!"

Sister Rita B. of West Palm Beach, Florida, swears that this story is true, and Saint Anthony would, no doubt, love it. A first-grader in a Catholic school was upset as he approached the cafeteria cashier at lunch time.

"I lost my dime for milk," he said, and began to cry.

"That's okay, honey," the cashier said kindly, "take some milk and have lunch, and when you're finished, go back outside and ask Saint Anthony to help you find your dime."

The tears continued. The boy said, "I can't. My mother said I couldn't talk to strangers!"

Some Cows for a New Diamond Engagement Ring

When Ann and Les F. of Glendo, Wyoming, were first married, they didn't have much money, so Les bought Ann a small diamond engagement ring.

"We had seven children," Ann said, "and somewhere washing all the diapers I lost the set out of the ring."

Several wedding anniversaries later, Les—that romantic devil—secretly sold some cows from the farm to buy Ann a new diamond ring. The diamond was no tiny sparkler this time, it was about half a carat.

One day, Ann and Les were driving to a funeral and Ann's ring snagged on her slacks. She glanced at the ring, and the diamond was gone. "I was devastated," Ann said, "because it meant so much to Les that I have a nice ring. So we prayed to Saint Anthony to find it."

Six months went by, and Ann gave up hope of ever finding the diamond. Still, she awoke one morning and prayed again to Saint Anthony to find the diamond. "And then I said, 'But how do I know you are even there if you can't find the diamond for me?'"

Ann got out of bed to dress, and as the sun shone through the bedroom's east window she saw a shiny object on the rug by her dresser. She picked it up and was amazed to see her diamond.

"This was nearly impossible," Ann said, "because I had vacuumed that rug many times since I lost the diamond. I can only give credit to Saint Anthony. Diamonds have never meant that much to me, it was just that Les wanted me to have a nice ring and went to so much trouble to get it for me. Maybe Saint Anthony took so long because it was just a material thing. Who knows?"

"I Won't Be Able to Visit My Husband!"

In the early 1950s, Frances O. of Orlando, Florida, was newly married and working in New York City, staying with her parents in New Jersey while her husband worked for a few months in North Carolina. Looking forward to a visit with her husband in North Carolina, Frances cashed her paycheck in order to make the trip.

Arriving home from work in the middle of a snow storm, Frances ran the block from the bus stop to her parents' home. Shortly thereafter, she looked for her wallet in her purse. It was gone. Retracing her steps back to the bus stop, the snow and dark made it impossible to see much of anything.

"The whole family prevailed upon Saint Anthony," Frances recalled.

The next morning, there was a knock on the door. There stood a neighbor who had been shoveling snow off the sidewalk near his house. "He had found my wallet intact," Frances said.

Saint Anthony, the Guiding Angel

In the early 1980s, the husband of the same Frances O., from the preceding story, ordered a new hearing aid. The hearing aid specialist gave Frances's husband a "loaner" to use until his new one was ready, cautioning him to take care of it because it was worth several hundred dollars.

"For some reason we can't recall now," Frances said, "he put the 'loaner' hearing aid in his shirt pocket."

Frances's husband left for the gas station and the chain-saw store, and when he returned he began to cut fire wood in the couple's back yard. Suddenly, he discovered that he had lost the "loaner" hearing aid.

Back he went to the gas station and the chain-saw store, searching for the valuable hearing aid. No luck.

"When I came home from work," Frances said, "and learned what had happened, I prevailed upon Saint Anthony to find the missing hearing aid."

Frances went out to the back yard, and for no particular reason picked up a small stick and waved it through the saw dust, looking randomly for the hearing aid. "In a few minutes it appeared," she said. "I never tire of reliving these incidents, and I truly believe that Saint Anthony is my guiding angel."

The Beads My Dead Son Gave Me Are Gone!

Olive S. and her husband had six healthy children—"a boisterous lot, for the most part," said her daughter-in-law, Shirley S. of Port Charlotte, Florida. But the second of the children, George, was "special, *very* special," Shirley said. "He was unusually devout."

George served as an altar boy at Saint Mary's, his family's parish church, often at the early Mass on Sunday mornings.

After that Mass, he would wait around, and if some boy failed to show up he would gladly serve another Mass.

Once, when the parish had a week-long mission, religious goods were sold and George bought his mother some simple rosary beads. "They were only large brown beans," Shirley said, "maybe coffee beans or something similar."

The following summer, George went swimming one day with some other boys, although he had a small cut on his leg. The cut developed a streptococcal infection, and because antibiotics that could have saved his life didn't exist yet, he soon died.

Olive treasured the simple rosary beads her son had given her. One morning she attended Mass, walked to the front of the church to receive Communion, and when she returned to her pew her purse was gone. Someone had stolen it. Olive reported the theft to the priest, but he could only caution the other women of the parish to hold tightly to their purses, even in church.

Heartbroken, Olive posted a notice in the vestibule of the church begging the thief to keep her money but to please return the rosary George had given her. "She also stormed the gates of heaven with her prayers," Shirley said. "She begged Saint Anthony to intercede with Almighty God...to find those simple rosary beads so very precious to her."

Three months went by with no results, and Olive became bitter. Why had Saint Anthony failed her? Still, she was a woman of integrity, and finally Olive decided to "accept her cross." She told her parish priest she had decided she must not be much of a Catholic if she couldn't even accept God's will in this matter. After this, she was a peace.

Hurrying up the street to her home and family, Olive heard the phone ringing as she opened the front door. The parish priest, known as a calm man, excitedly told her a strange tale. After he finished hearing confessions that evening, he went to lock the back door of the church, and there, hanging on the end of the last pew, was a woman's purse. It was Olive's purse! The money was gone—in fact everything that had been in the purse was gone, except the rosary George had given his mother. After more than three months, this was incredible.

"I married Olive's oldest son, Joe," Shirley said. "Years went by, and ultimately Joe and I had the sad task of burying his devoted mother. We placed the old, simple, well-worn brown rosary beads in her hands to hold for all eternity in her earthly grave. No doubt her soul is safe in heaven with Almighty God...the always faithful Saint Anthony, and her beloved son, George."

"I Lost Jim, but I Don't Want to Lose His Diamond!"

In 1957, Joyce B. of Spokane, Washington, became engaged to Jim, a U.S. Air Force pilot. Two months before they were to be married, Jim was killed in a plane crash. Joyce continued to wear the engagement ring Jim had given her until she met Howard, her future husband. After she and Howard were married, he had the stones remounted into a dinner ring so she could continue to wear it on her right hand and not have to answer anymore painful questions about it.

"One day in the mid-1970s," Joyce said, "I looked down at my hand and the large diamond was gone." She immediately asked Saint Anthony for help in deciding what to do. The parish Joyce grew up in was named for Saint Anthony, so she felt that she and the saint had a long-term relationship. After much prayer and deliberation, she decided that if she ever wanted to see the diamond again—"God helps those who help themselves"—she had better get busy and vacuum the house methodically.

"Howard thought I had lost my mind," Joyce said. "He said I'd never find it in this big house. I even vacuumed the garage and the cars."

Bag after bag from the vacuum cleaner Joyce emptied on

a screen, more bags than she could remember. "The last thing to drop out of the last bag was the diamond! I really can't express in words my devotion to Saint Anthony since that day."

Joyce told this story to others over the years, and some criticized her for praying for something so materialistic. "My response has always been: 'I lost my Jim but if I can help it I certainly do not want to lose his diamond!' "

Christopher Is Lost

Her shopping completed, Mary left a shopping mall in Florence, South Carolina, her eight-year-old son, Johnny, in tow. She had bought Johnny a new pair of shoes. On their way out, said Mary's mother, Maureen M. of Oyster Bay, New York, Mary and her son passed a distraught mother who was explaining to a security guard that her son, Christopher, had wandered away. He was two and a half years old; he was blond, he was wearing a T-shirt with words on it about being a brother, or something. Mary didn't hear all of what the other woman said to the security officer.

The eyes of the two mothers met briefly, and Mary shared the other woman's fear and anxiety. Mary wondered if she should have stopped to offer help. As she kept walking, she said a quick prayer to Saint Anthony for help. *Isn't he the one to find lost things?* she wondered.

As Mary and her son left the mall, in front of them was a man, a young girl, and a little boy. The man and girl left, but the little boy remained behind. Mary noticed he was wearing a T-shirt which read, "I Am a Big Brother." He was blond. Mary said to the little boy, "Are you Christopher?" He replied, "Yes."

Taking him by the hand, Mary led Christopher back into the mall telling him his mother was very upset that he had gone off without her; he must never do that again. Another lady overheard the conversation and asked, "Is that Christopher?" "Yes," Mary replied.

By this time, Christopher and his mother saw each other and were running toward a reunion. Mary and Johnny turned and left the mall. Johnny asked, "How did you know that was Christopher?"

"I heard them talking, and Saint Anthony did the rest," Mary replied.

Where Is Louis XIV?

In the mid-1980s, Maureen M. of Oyster Bay, New York, was editor of a small weekly newspaper. Edwina, the publisher, was without a car one day and asked Maureen to drive her and her granddaughter, Lorin, home from a school play. It was the Christmas season and a rainy day.

Maureen learned that her publisher's basset hound, Louis XIV, had been missing for quite a while. It looked like a dognapping since it would have been difficult for the dog to wander far on his own. He was a mischievous pup and sometimes a nuisance to the neighbors.

Lorin was upset at the loss of Louis XIV, and on the ride home she talked about "Louie" and how much she missed him. Edwina said that she missed him, too, but she wasn't too hopeful because so much time had gone by since he disappeared. She said that if he didn't turn up in a week or two there would be no further hope.

Maureen asked if they had prayed to Saint Anthony for Louie's safe return. Lorin wanted to know why they hadn't done that. Edwina said, "Honey, we did pray…." But they had not prayed to Saint Anthony. After all, they were not Catholics.

"Saint Anthony always finds lost things," Maureen said. She told Edwina and her granddaughter about the time one of her sons had lost his wallet and was near panic. Maureen suggested he pray to Saint Anthony and look again where he thought he last had his wallet. A little while later he returned, wallet in hand, asking, "Who was that we prayed to?"

Another son lost his wallet one time in Manhattan. Maureen suggested prayer to Saint Anthony, and one day a post office employee phoned saying they had his wallet, would he pick it up? Someone sent it to the post office, without the money, but with all the important papers still intact.

As she drove home after dropping off Edwina and Lorin, Maureen spoke aloud to Saint Anthony. She told him how important this was and if ever he was going to help this was the time to do so. Once she was home, Maureen didn't think about Louis XIV again, and the weeks went by.

Answering the phone one day, Maureen heard a voice announce excitedly, without preliminaries, "It's a miracle!"

"What is?"

"It's a miracle!"

It was Edwina, and Maureen had no idea what she was talking about. She didn't even think about the dog.

"Louie! He's been found! It's a miracle!"

Mysteriously, at the eastern end of Long Island, miles from his Centre Island home, Louis XIV was rescued from a dog pound. He was scheduled to be "put to sleep" the next day. Someone who had read the story about the missing dog in the *Oyster Bay Guardian* was visiting a friend in the village of Saint James who knew about the stray-but-pedigreed Louis XIV and what was going to happen to him the next day.

Someone at the pound called Edwina, and she retrieved Louie the same day. He was a mere shadow of his former self, but Louis XIV all the same.

"Somehow," Maureen said, "Saint Anthony had put the whole thing together at the nth hour."

A Treasured Pearl

For years, Margaret N. of Chicago, Illinois, treasured a gold necklace with a few gold charms on it, including a pearl encased in a gold shell. The pearl was especially significant to her because Margaret means "pearl." One day, Margaret noticed that the pearl from her necklace was gone.

"So," Margaret said, "I asked Saint Anthony for help, which I had learned from my mother to do when something is lost."

Three days later, Margaret went down to the basement of her house to do the laundry. She bent down to pick something up and rising bumped her head on the laundry chute. "Right there on the floor was my pearl," Margaret said. "I said, 'Thank you, Saint Anthony!' It was like he was saying, 'It's right there, you dummy! Just look.'

"So, I got my pearl back with help from Saint Anthony."

"My Pocketbook Was Burglarized"

One day, Catherine L. of Breezy Point, New York, found that her pocketbook had been taken from her home by a burglar. She said a prayer to Saint Anthony, asking him to find it for her.

"It was a miracle to me," Catherine said, "when my neighbor was working in his garden and found my bag. The thief took only the money. All my pictures and other valuables were still there. More things are wrought by prayer than this world dreams of."

Saint Anthony and a Scuba Diver

Carol and Mike S. of Seattle, Washington, spend some time every August vacationing on the shores of north-central Washington State's Lake Chelan. The couple spent their honeymoon there, so it is a special place for them on that account, as well. In 1992, Carol and Mike had "a close encounter of the Saint Anthony kind" while staying at Lake Chelan.

"Mike's a jock," Carol said, "and if someone's throwing a ball of any kind he's there. He threw the football and with the football went his wedding ring."

Carol looked up from her beach recliner and saw Mike down in the water, thigh deep, looking for something in the lake. She called out, "What are you looking for?" Mike casually replied, "My wedding ring." "What?!!" Carol exclaimed. "He knew I'd have a breakdown."

Each morning for the next four days, Carol, Mike, and helpful friends and acquaintances searched for Mike's wedding ring. Lake Chelan is sandy, so they knew the ring must have sunk just below the surface of the sand.

Carol immediately began to call on Saint Anthony to help find Mike's wedding ring. They even hired scuba divers to join the search, but the ring seemed gone forever.

The day before Carol and Mike were scheduled to return to their home in Seattle, Carol went to the local pawnshop to tell them about Mike's ring. "In the fall," she said, "the water level of the lake drops, and the locals head down to the beach with metal detectors. Mike's ring was engraved and had a date on it, so it would be easy to identify."

As Carol was talking to the owner of the pawnshop and giving her their phone number, in walked a young man who overheard what was going on. He told Carol that he was a scuba diver and had an extremely sensitive metal detector. "I dive for lost jewelry in Hawaii," he said.

The young scuba diver was passing through Chelan and happened to be in the same little pawnshop when Carol was there. She arranged with the scuba diver to meet the next morning before she and Mike left for home. "Saint Anthony was still my only thought most of the day," Carol said.

The next morning, the scuba diver dove into the lake with

his metal detector, near the spot where Mike thought his ring plopped into the water. The couple watched anxiously as the search went on for nearly an hour.

"All of a sudden," Carol said, "he comes up out of the water and holds up the ring. 'Ta-da!' he said. The people on the beach were clapping and cheering. I said, 'Thank you, Saint Anthony, thank you!' I just knew he had done it."

A Canadian Crisis

One day, Raeanna M. of Falls Church, Virginia, lost her wallet. "I am Canadian," she explained, "and naturally I had my driver's license and work permit and other important papers in my wallet. To replace these things would have taken a great deal of time, money, and frustration."

Raeanna prayed to Saint Anthony and looked everywhere for her wallet. After a week of looking—"and still trusting in Saint Anthony"—she pleaded saying, "Saint Anthony, on the feast of All Saints"—coming in a few days—"please help me to find my lost wallet."

On the feast of All Saints, November 1, Raeanna found her wallet in her car, where she had already looked "several times."

"Get Off Your Ass, Saint Anthony!"

Mary O. died at the age of ninety-six, in 1985. Her son, Edward O. of Midland, Michigan, said that his mother—at the time the oldest living member of her 1913 class at the University of Michigan—was a great devotee of Saint Anthony. "She had a lifelong relationship with Saint Anthony," Ed said, "which I grew to suspect as rather superstitious."

A year-and-a-half before her death, Mary misplaced her magnifying glass, which had a cord attached so she could put it around her neck for help with reading. Mary prayed frequently for two days with no results. Finally, Ed said, "relying on a long relationship with Saint Anthony, she shouted, 'Look here Saint Anthony, you have had enough time on this request. Damn it! Get off your ass and find it!'"

No sooner had she spoken, Ed said, than "the missing magnifying glass appeared."

"Have You Lost Anything Recently?"

After returning from a shopping trip, Sister M. Charlotte G. of Chicago, Illinois, discovered that a plastic case holding her Medicare card, Blue Cross/Blue Shield papers, and other important cards had disappeared from her purse. "I searched for days," she said, "in every possible place hoping to find the case had slipped into some pocket or box, yet it seemed these important items were irretrievably lost."

Sister M. Charlotte said that "naturally" she had appealed many times to Saint Anthony to help find her lost documents and cards, "but he seemed deaf to my plea and I gave them up as definitely gone."

Nearly two months passed, and one day another member of Sister M. Charlotte's religious community asked, "Have you lost anything recently?" Sister told her the story of her lost cards and about how hard she had prayed.

"Well," the other Sister said, "here is your case with all the cards intact." As the other Sister packed some items to send to the Salvation Army, she found an old blue clutch bag Sister M. Charlotte had donated. She checked through the three pockets in the little bag, and at the very bottom she found the plastic case firmly wedged into the crease. Recognizing Sister M. Charlotte's name on the cards, she recalled hearing Sister mention "praying to Saint Anthony to find something that was lost."

"Here was my answer once again," Sister M. Charlotte said, "to prayers said to my friend, the 'Finder of Lost Articles.'"

Six Golden Cups and Saucers

One of the most treasured possessions of Adele C. of Bayside, New York, was "a beautiful neckpiece of the Blessed Mother." When this neckpiece was lost one day, Adele searched her home methodically with no success.

"One day I was determined to search the house with diligence," she said. "I looked in all my purses, coats, suits…. Nothing turned up. It was at this time I said a prayer to Saint Anthony asking him to guide or lead me to wherever the neckpiece was."

Adele "instantly" went to her dining room "which has two dish closets." For no particular reason, she skipped the first closet and went to the second where she kept six golden cup-and-saucer sets.

"I put my hand in the first cup, second cup, third cup—nothing. I lifted the third cup—and I found my precious neckpiece. I have no recollection of ever putting it there."

"I Only Prayed to Him Because I Was Desperate"

Martha M.'s glasses had been missing for two days, and the Brooklyn, New York, woman was at wit's end. A friend encouraged her to pray to Saint Anthony, so she did, but, she said, "to me he was just another saint on the calendar." Given Martha's lack of familiarity with Saint Anthony, you can imagine why she was "surprised, delighted, amazed, and even a little frightened" when she found her eyeglasses. "I only prayed to him because I was desperate and my friend insisted that he would help me."

The autumn weather was horrendous, rain coming down in sheets, a strong wind blowing all the leaves off the trees in a matter of minutes. "It was so bad," Martha recalled, "that the sewers and streets became flooded."

Martha had an appointment at a beauty salon, and since the weather seemed to let up, she decided to keep the appointment. Besides, the optometrist's office was only two blocks from the beauty salon. Despairing of ever seeing her glasses again, she decided this would be a convenient time to order new ones.

As Martha left the beauty salon, however, it started to drizzle. "I decided to go home instead of going to the optometrist's office," she said, "before it started to really rain again."

As she walked toward home, Martha felt silly for asking a saint to find her glasses. Then she began to think that she should have gone to the optometrist after all. "I wagged my finger in the air and said out loud, 'But Saint Anthony, I wanted to give you one more chance.'"

With that, Martha looked down in order to hop over a puddle covered with leaves, and there at her feet were her glasses. She was shocked. "I had been searching up and down that street for two days, so I couldn't believe my eyes. I had to look twice to make sure I wasn't seeing things."

Picking up her glasses, Martha ran "jumping and shouting" into her friend's home. "I found my glasses!" she exclaimed.

Of course, she had to listen to "I told you so" for two weeks, but it was worth it to Martha. Since that time she has become "a friend of Saint Anthony," and he has helped her many times. "The most important," she said, "was helping my son find a job." For that story, read on....

A Lost Needle in the Grass

Elizabeth O. of Owensboro, Kentucky, considers Saint Anthony her "protector."

"Many years ago, I was sitting on the back-porch steps sewing and watching my four young children play in the yard,"

Elizabeth said. "When it was time to go in, I stood up and inadvertently dropped my needle in the grass. I searched and searched, but I could not find it. I cautioned my children to be very careful walking in the yard for fear they might step on it."

Knowing the danger a lost needle can cause, Elizabeth immediately began praying to Saint Anthony to help her find it. Later that evening, Elizabeth and her children were once again in the back yard. "I wanted to show them how it was possible to whistle by blowing through a blade of grass held between their thumbs," she recalls. "I pulled a blade of grass from the yard and there was the needle stuck in the one blade I had chosen. Saint Anthony's heavenly power once again provided us with his merciful protection."

"He Didn't Know Where He Was Going"

The son of Martha M. had finished college two years ago, and still he had not found a good job. "He didn't know where he was going or even know what he wanted to do." He had a part-time job working from midnight to 8:00 A.M., and that was it.

Every Tuesday for three months, Martha attended Mass as a novena to Saint Anthony, asking him to help her son find a good job, and after a year he found a full-time position with a brokerage firm. After two years there, he and two other young men decided to take a chance and open their own brokerage business.

"He is now making a six-figure salary," Martha said. "Sometimes, even with the help of Saint Anthony, things don't happen immediately."

Martha said that her stories "may not be spectacular happenings to anyone else," but they have changed her life.

"We Felt That There Is Strength in Numbers"

In the late 1970s, Mary Joan L. of Chicago, Illinois, was in the middle of a teaching career that lasted for thirty-one years. Teaching fourth grade at Pulaski School, in Chicago, she noticed one day that Ruth G., a fellow teacher across the hall from her classroom, was upset. Ruth said that she had lost her gold wedding ring and couldn't find it anywhere. She had been married, Mary Joan said, for more than twenty years, "so it was practically a part of her anatomy."

Perhaps, Mary Joan suggested, Ruth had been losing weight and the ring had inadvertently fallen off. At any rate, Ruth had searched everywhere for her wide gold wedding band, all over her classroom, in her car, and at home, with no happy outcome.

"Ruth is Jewish," Mary Joan explained, "and a believer." Still, Mary Joan told Ruth about Saint Anthony, explaining that one prays to him to find lost items. She also told another teacher, Mary K., who ran the computer lab, and her aide, Elizabeth M. "Since we felt that there is strength in numbers, we all three prayed for the recovery of Ruth's ring."

A week went by, and still no wedding ring. "Ruth had just about lost hope," Mary Joan said.

The school janitor, Rich R., also knew about the lost ring. He had helped Ruth to look for it in her classroom. One day down in the school's boiler room, Rich looked through a waste basket full of papers, and there he found the lost gold band. Ruth could hardly believe it when Rich handed it to her.

"What was so remarkable," Mary Joan said, "is the long time-lapse that had occurred." Waste paper was usually burned in the incinerator within a matter of hours. That a waste basket—and specifically the one from Ruth's classroom—should go unemptied for so long was very unusual.

Saint Anthony's Tomb

The same Mary Joan L. said that in 1960, just after her first year of teaching, she went on a two-month tour of Europe with a college group. "We went to many countries and saw many shrines and other famous places," she said.

A special memory for Mary Joan is her visit to the tomb of Saint Anthony in Padua, Italy. "It was a large stone sarcophagus. I remember putting my hand on the side, and it felt alive, like an atomic pile. It just [felt] very powerful."

"I Sure Do Need Those Sunglasses"

Living in Seattle, Washington, Rita M. needs an umbrella more often than she needs sunglasses—but when she needs them she needs them!

Rita could not find her sunglasses, search where she might. "This was the second pair I had lost in a short time," she said, "so I was reluctant to purchase new ones. I searched everywhere and prayed to Saint Anthony daily."

Along came a bright, sunny day, and Rita needed those sunglasses. "I said, 'Saint Anthony, I sure do need my sunglasses today.' "

As Rita got into her car, she glanced in the back seat, and there were her sunglasses in plain sight in the middle of the seat. "The day before," she said, "I had ridden in the back seat as my granddaughter and her friend were in the front. There were no glasses there at that time."

Dad Turned It Over to Saint Anthony

Now in her seventies, Mary B. of Seattle, Washington, said that when she was eleven years old she was "profoundly impressed" by her father's unshakable faith in the help of his favorite saint, Saint Anthony.

"Dad loved to attend baseball games," Mary said, and often on a Sunday he went to cheer for Seattle's minor league team, in those days the Seattle Rainiers. Mary's father owned and operated a neighborhood grocery store during the Great Depression, and times being what they were he was, she said, "just able to keep afloat, with little margin between profit and loss."

Mary's father could ill afford to lose any money, "although he seldom refused credit to any mother of a family who needed food for her children and had no money to pay."

One Sunday—his only day off—Mary's dad took his family to the ball park to watch the Rainiers play. While there, somehow he lost his wallet containing, Mary said, "quite a bit of money from his Saturday store receipts."

Everyone but Mary's father was upset. He "turned it over to Saint Anthony."

Nearly a week went by with no news of the wallet. The subject came up at the dinner table, Mary said, "and Dad still maintained Saint Anthony would come through, although the rest of us were making negative comments like, 'You'd better kiss that one good-bye!'"

At the very moment his family was poking fun at him for expecting to hear anything about his wallet, the phone rang. Mary's father answered. "A man called to say he had found the wallet," Mary recalled, "and had just been too busy to get back to him."

The man brought the wallet to Mary's father with all the money and everything else still in it, and he refused to accept any reward.

"You can believe," Mary said, "that having witnessed the results of absolute faith, I still resort to the good offices of Dad's favorite saint."

A Lost Miraculous Medal

Mrs. John L. of Brooklyn, New York, said that one day she lost a beautiful gold Miraculous Medal, which she had worn for years. Mrs. L. misplaced the medal one day and "was heartsick over the loss."

Two or three weeks went by, and Mrs. L. prayed daily asking Saint Anthony to help her find the medal. Then one day she was out in her backyard, walking across the lawn. She looked down and could not believe her eyes. "There was my medal sticking up out of the grass, although the chain was missing."

Mrs. L. "immediately started prayers of thanksgiving to Saint Anthony" for what "was like a miracle to me."

Where Can My Jewelry Be?

"I was never a particular devotee of Saint Anthony," said Mrs. Maurice M. of Cohasset, Massachusetts, "until about twenty years ago." Then a friend told Mrs. M. about her love for Saint Anthony "and how he never forgot his own on earth."

Upon hearing this, Mrs. M. told her friend that she had been searching for two years for some rather valuable jewelry. Each year, when she and her husband went to spend the summer at their summer home, she would put her jewelry in a safe-deposit box. One July Mrs. M.'s husband died unexpectedly.

"I returned to New York," Mrs. M. said, "and there was no special occasion when I wanted my jewelry, until Christmas." She wanted to wear her engagement ring and a certain necklace but they were nowhere to be found, not even in the safe-deposit box. Where had she put the jewelry?

"I fudged my appearance," Mrs. M. said, "if anyone, particularly my children, should ask."

It was several years before Mrs. M.'s friend told her of her devotion to Saint Anthony. "She was extolling him and his love for troubled humanity." So Mrs. M. told her about her lost jewelry, and her friend said that Saint Anthony was particularly fond of the needy. Mrs. M. decided that if Saint Anthony helped her to find her jewelry she would show her gratitude by making a donation to a good cause for the poor.

"Mentally, I said, 'There's five hundred dollars for you, dear saint.' Then I forgot the whole business except for calling his attention to this at Mass each morning."

Some months later, Mrs. M. saw a plea in a magazine or newspaper for help for a residence for sick and retired priests. "I tore it out, put it on the front of my dresser, and promised I'd send something on my return to New York, where my home had been sold." It was waiting to be cleared out.

It was July, stifling hot, especially in a closed-up three-story brownstone. Mrs. M. decided to start on the third floor and work her way down. The closets had two high shelves, and after clearing out two rooms she decided to take on a third. The second shelf in this room was full of an assortment of things that looked like they should have been thrown out years ago, so that is what Mrs. M. proceeded to do. "Most of it was junk indeed, and into the trash bag it went, including a box marked 'Old Christmas Cards.'"

It was Mrs. M.'s custom to save the Christmas cards received each year and then to mail them the next autumn to an orphanage where the children cut them up for Christmas decorations.

"'Oh, dear,' I said to myself, 'I guess I'll have to retrieve that box or the children will be disappointed.'" Reluctantly, feeling sorry for herself at the extra inconvenience this would mean, she retrieved the box from the rubbish and idly opened it. There was her jewelry case. Suddenly she remembered that the last time she and her husband had been packing to leave for their summer home she decided to put the jewelry case in the box with the old Christmas cards, instead of in the safe-deposit box as she usually did. "I was in a great hurry that time, and I thought that I would be sending the cards to the children, so I would open the box, and my jewelry would be right at hand for the season." Instead, Mrs. M. completely forgot she had done that.

When Mrs. M. found her jewelry after almost throwing it out with the trash, she was alone. "There was nobody to tell it to except Saint Anthony. As soon as I got home," she said, "I mailed the check to the residence for sick and retired priests." Mrs. M. enclosed a letter explaining what had happened, "and they were delighted and amused. Everyone was happy, especially myself."

Mrs. M. said that she thanks "the dear saint" every day after Mass, "and I tell him I expect nothing big ever again, but please to keep tabs on my glasses and myself."

"Come On, Tony. It Can't Just Walk Away!"

Part of the normal grief process, said Martha T. of Park Forest, Illinois, is a period called "the crazies." In 1982, Martha's husband Norm died suddenly. "I went through the wake and funeral sustained by the shock of sudden loss," she said. "Christmas followed soon after, and I managed to stay glued together."

In January, however, Martha started losing things—her car keys, gloves, books for a class she was taking, and other objects, as well. "I must have prayed to Saint Anthony for specific lost items ten or twelve times a day. A friend who had a similar experience said she is now on a nickname basis with him. She just says, 'Tony, help!' " Now Martha does the same.

One day, Martha couldn't find a ring her husband gave her. The ring wasn't particularly valuable, but Norm bought it for her in an antique shop because it looked a lot like one that had belonged to her grandmother. That sentimental gesture meant as much to Martha as the ring itself.

"I remembered taking it off and putting it in a drawer," Martha said. "I blamed it on 'the crazies.' It wasn't in the nightstand. It wasn't in the jewelry box. I prayed to Saint Anthony as I dug through the vacuum-cleaner bag. It wasn't there, either."

Martha all but gave up hope of finding the ring. She tried to put it out of her mind, but she couldn't. Every time she thought of it she brought it to "Tony's" attention. "As my mom used to say, it couldn't have walked away."

Four years went by, and Martha still hoped Saint Anthony would help her find her ring. Preparing to move, she packed books from bookshelves and her nightstand. She passed a dustcloth over the books before she put them in a box. Suddenly, she felt the cloth catch on something, and there in the dustcloth was her ring Norm gave her. "It had fallen behind the drawer and gotten caught in a book."

Four years, Martha said, and "Tony hadn't let me down."

Martha added that on many occasions Saint Anthony was not so slow to act. "All those keys, gloves, and books that were lost. The brand-new earring that I found a minute after a friend walked by and said he'd pray to Saint Anthony for me. The rosary, also a gift from my husband, that was missing because I couldn't remember where I set it down—that was another one that took awhile, but I never gave up on it. Each time it came to mind I'd say a prayer."

Whenever something is lost, Martha said, she prays, "Come on Tony, they have to be here. They can't just walk away!"

No Keys, No Service!

Bru M. of Jackson Heights, New York, recalled the beginning of her devotion to Saint Anthony when she witnessed him at work with her pastor, Monsignor John D. Each Monday evening, Monsignor D. led a short devotional service in the parish church. When Bru arrived, he stood outside the church doors and told her that he had misplaced the keys to the church.

"He invoked Saint Anthony for help," Bru said, "and in a short time he was led to find his keys."

Saint Anthony Delivers...by UPS

Studying in Rome in 1993, Sister Paula M. received word from her sister that their mother in Chicago sent her a package for Christmas via United Parcel Service. Sister Paula's sister shipped the package the week before Thanksgiving, but it did not arrive in time for Christmas.

Sister Paula's mother inquired with UPS about the whereabouts of the package, but the UPS people told her that nothing could be done to trace the package until it had been missing for ninety days. Sister Paula said a prayer to Saint Anthony.

Soon thereafter, as Sister Paula left the library where she had been studying, she saw a UPS truck, the first she had seen in Rome. "I laughed," she said. Then, on her way home she met another Sister who told her that her package had just arrived.

"It's a small, simple thing," Sister Paula said. "However, I always will be convinced of the power of Saint Anthony's loving care."

Lost in the Fourth Floor Ladies Room

In 1993, a coworker of Terri R. of Queens Village, New York, lost a treasured ring in the ladies room on the fourth floor of the building they work in. "We all thought for sure the ring was gone forever," Terri said. "All except Catherine, who prayed to Saint Anthony."

More than two weeks went by, and to everyone's astonishment the ring showed up in a cabinet on the fifth floor. "Even stranger," Terri said, "the person who found it approached Catherine, of all people, to ask what to do with it." Catherine returned the ring to the coworker, who was overjoyed.

Terri said that she heard of many cases in which Catherine was involved in praying to Saint Anthony "with much success of returned items. I believe she has a strong faith."

A couple of months later, Terri's husband, a high-school teacher, lost his new glasses. "It was the first time in his life he had decided to get nice ones, and they cost a good deal of money," Terri said. "We could not really afford to replace them at the time."

Terri and her husband both thought of Catherine's "remarkable faith," and they asked her help in praying to Saint Anthony for the return of the glasses. Catherine called the next day to see if the glasses had been found. "I replied no," Terri said, "and explained that they were most likely taken by a student." Catherine said she would pray that the student would have a change of heart.

Terri thanked Catherine, and the weeks went by with her husband wearing his old glasses. Catherine kept reminding Terri and her husband that sometimes it takes time.

"Then it happened," Terri said. "My husband phoned me at work and said another teacher had found his glasses on a desk in a classroom."

The glasses were mangled, but repairable at little cost, and the lenses were undamaged. "I told Catherine, and we were so excited we hugged, and I thanked her repeatedly. She said, 'Don't thank me, thank Saint Anthony.'"

The License Was Lost, Not the Dog

In 1990, Rose Marie R. and her daughter, of Manalapan, New Jersey, went to buy licenses for their two dogs and for two of their six cats. They also wanted to get rabies shots for the dogs. "I bought the licenses," Rose said, "and we left."

On the way home, Rose and her daughter decided to stop at a store for milk, and in all the excitement of handling cats and dogs, they realized that they could not find the licenses they had just bought. Rose said a quick prayer to Saint Anthony, and they went into the store.

"When we came back out and got into the car," Rose recalled, "next to me on the floor were the licenses. Before we went into the store we both looked high and low, on the floor of the car and everyplace, but we could not find those licenses. I feel it was Saint Anthony who found them for me."

Where Were Dad's Insurance Papers?

Nancy K.'s father was dying of cancer, slowly and painfully. The Sonora, California, woman was visiting the home of her mother and father after being on her own for nearly ten years.

"Mom was looking for Dad's insurance papers so all would be in order when the time came," Nancy explained. "They were not where they had always been kept."

Nancy and her mother prayed to Saint Anthony, asking the saint for help in finding the important papers. "Within minutes it came to me," Nancy said, "to look in a bedroom closet, on a particular shelf, and there the papers were, mixed in with old newspaper clippings, recipes, and so forth, where there was no rhyme or reason for them to be. Also, there was no reason for me to have any knowledge of where they were."

After returning home, Nancy prayed that Saint Anthony would intercede with God to either cure her father or take him, he was suffering so much. When the phone call came a few weeks later informing Nancy that her father had died, she looked to see what day it was on the Catholic liturgical calendar. "Dad had died early in the morning on June 13," Nancy said, "Saint Anthony's feast day."

After this, Nancy said, Saint Anthony became her "good

heavenly friend to whom I turn for intercession in spiritual and physical problems."

"I Felt a Sadness That Made My Bones Ache"

Bob R., an international professional bicycle racer, writing in *VeloNews* magazine, told of losing a wrist watch given to him by a cosponsor of a racing team he belonged to. "Not just any watch," he wrote, "but a TAG Heuer titanium-and-gold piece of exquisite Swiss art."

Looking at his watch, Bob could remember dozens of races he wore the watch in, and many of the interesting and exotic places he visited as a cyclist. "That watch exploded off Tour de France prologue time trial ramps from Paris to Berlin.... That watch's crystal face glistened with citric acid from the peels of blood oranges in desolate hilltop Sicilian towns, and mirrored the vision of my jagged teeth turned crimson from the juice of the orange.... It was splashed with holy water in Lourdes...."

On January 13, 1993, Bob and two friends went back-country snowboarding, high in some mountains. "I wanted to improve my descending rhythm," Bob said, "for the up-coming mountain-bike season."

After a strenuous day of climbing and gliding down snowy slopes, Bob and his friends decided to call it quits. "When we got to the car and started to load up," Bob recalled, "I realized I had lost my bloody watch. I let out an anguished scream to the heavens, as I looked back on a million square acres of ice."

Bob's friends suggested returning in the spring, after the snow had melted, to look for the watch, but Bob was beyond being comforted.

All winter, the snow continued to fall burying Bob's wrist watch deeper and deeper. "I hoped my watch was in suspended animation," Bob said, "ticking away just as it had done from

Oakland to Oostende...but I realized the chances of finding it were reduced to slim and none...."

On April 7, Bob returned to where he lost his watch, only to find there was still ten feet of snow. He returned again on May 15 with his wife, Chiara. At first he was hopeful, the ground was clear and he could see every square inch. Then he began to wonder. Was this even the right place? Everything had changed so much in appearance since the snow melted. At one point, Bob almost killed himself when he slipped on an icy snow patch and "accelerated to terminal velocity toward a drop-off, before being halted by a thorn-vine-wrapped scrub oak tree."

Finally, Bob cried aloud, "All right, that is it!" He began to walk back to his car "in anger and despair." He followed the path he had taken earlier in the day, back down to the highway, not ready to give up completely, but trying to be realistic.

"As the words of Saint Anthony lit up my mind," Bob wrote, "as I tried to remember the patron saint of all things lost, just as my wife pointed to a circling red-tailed hawk above my head...there it was. Glistening like a diamond on a mountain of coal dust, my watch smiled up at me from a patch of snow."

"I Remembered the Five-Year-Old Boy Who Had Drowned"

On a blistering hot day in July 1945, Patrick and Clara B., of Commodore, Pennsylvania, took their four sons—ages four months to seven years—to go swimming at Rockaway Beach, New Jersey. "The sand on the beach was so hot it was almost painful to walk on it," Patrick recalled. "The crowd was so dense you had to push your way through it to get near the surf."

Later in the day, when Patrick and Clara decided it was

time to head for home, they discovered that Jimmy, hardly more than a toddler, was nowhere to be found. "We felt he could not be far away for the sand would scorch his feet and he would be right back."

Minutes passed, and there was no sign of Jimmy. Leaving the baby in the care of the two older boys, Patrick and Clara set out in opposite directions, alerting lifeguards along the way to look for him. "We retraced our steps up and down a long stretch of the beach," Patrick said, "with the surf booming in our ears."

Patrick recalled that just a week before, as a member of the Harbor Precinct of the New York Police Department, he retrieved from the waters of the East River the body of a five-year-old boy who had fallen from the sea wall and drowned. "The memory of that little fellow's hair floating on the top of the oily water still stays with me," he said. "I could picture our Jimmy carried beyond the surf."

On the verge of despair, Clara finally returned to her other three boys. She went down on her knees in the sand and prayed, "Dear Saint Anthony, please find our Jimmy."

Remaining on her knees for half a minute or so, suddenly Clara looked up and saw a woman pushing her way through the crowd with Jimmy's hand in hers.

One Lost Turtle

Mary P. of Brooklyn, New York, explained to her grandson, age seven, that if you lose something and pray to Saint Anthony, you will find it again. "He listened," she said, "and one day I called him, and he told me he lost his turtle."

Mary reminded her grandson that Saint Anthony is the saint to pray to when you lose something.

The following day the boy called his grandmother and said, "I found my turtle. It really works. But, you know what, Saint Anthony didn't find it. I did."

Where Could a Wedding Ring Be?

One evening, after bedding down six children, Jane G. of Springfield, Illinois, finished the kitchen chores, made sure the front door was locked, turned out the living-room lights, patted the family's Irish wolfhound who slept by the door, and walked through the kitchen toward her and her husband's bedroom.

"I looked in the dining room where I usually left my wedding ring while cleaning up. It wasn't there. I looked in the dining room, the bathroom, and finally enlisted my husband's help."

While Jane's husband looked in all the likely places he could think of, Jane went to the library-cum-recreation room. Not finding the ring, she said to Saint Anthony, "Look—if you find this ring for me I won't have any alcoholic drink for thirty days."

"At that moment," Jane said, "—word of honor—my husband called, 'I found it!' I had put my ring in my shirt pocket, and when I leaned down to pat the wolfhound it had fallen onto his rug."

Jane and her husband counted out the thirty days she owed Saint Anthony, and the thirtieth day was June 13, Saint Anthony's feast day.

"My Wrist Watch Slipped Off My Wrist"

One day, as Sally S. of Cincinnati, Ohio, walked through a mall parking lot, her wrist watch slipped off her wrist without her realizing it. This wrist watch had special meaning for Sally because she had always worn it when she visited her seven-year-old son, Sammy, when he was in the hospital. Sammy died of cancer.

"When I realized it was gone," Sally said, "I walked through the lot toward the bank, seeking Saint Anthony's help in finding it. And there it was, lying in one of the driving lanes, intact."

"I Missed a Diamond Ring Which Had Been My Mother's"

While Robert and Irene W. prepared to move from their condo in California to a new home in Lake Oswego, Oregon, Irene discovered that a treasured keepsake was missing. "I missed a diamond ring which had been my mother's," Irene explained. "I was distraught but immediately asked Saint Anthony's help."

Irene walked outside to go to her and Robert's car—"and there on the sidewalk was my ring."

"I Accidentally Dropped My Hearing Aid"

In 1992, Father Amadeus B., a Franciscan priest living in Boston, Massachusetts, accompanied his brother and two sisters on a foliage-viewing trip throughout New England. One morning, as he stood before the desk in his motel room, he accidentally dropped his hearing aid, which was very expensive. "I got down on my knees and looked around and under the desk for the hearing aid," he said. "There was no sign of it."

After a while, Father Amadeus called on his brother and sisters to help look for the hearing aid, but their efforts proved fruitless, as well. "I was about to give up," he said, "when I, a Franciscan, decided to call on my fellow Franciscan, Saint Anthony of Padua, for assistance. I promised him a hundred dollars for his poor if he would help me to find the hearing aid."

The search continued with no results, so Father Amadeus decided to call off the search. But one of his sisters, Elizabeth, wanted to continue. The hearing aid had been there; it was dropped; it had to be someplace! Elizabeth stayed and kept looking, even after Father Amadeus left the room. Finally, she began to give up, too. Then, just before she closed the door of the room she glanced one more time at the area around the desk.

"She surprised us," Father Amadeus recalled, "by saying, 'Hey, look what I see!' Sure enough, there on the floor, about an inch in front of the desk, was my hearing aid! All I can say is that Saint Anthony has a way about him. And I faithfully and gladly kept my part of the bargain."

"My Son Lost His Contact Lens in the Snow"

"It was a nasty, miserable winter day," said Kathryn G. of Haddon Heights, New Jersey. "My younger son was wearing hard contact lenses, and he lost one of them in the deep snow."

Kathryn and her son walked from one end of the block to the other, looking into the snow. "I was saying a prayer to Saint Anthony," she said, "imploring him for help, when on the top of a snowbank was this tiny clear disc. How I ever managed to spot this lens was unbelievable. God bless Saint Anthony."

He Lost His Cousin's Play Action Figure in Grandma's Hedge

"I'm a latecomer to the ranks of Saint Anthony believers," said John Paul A., of Los Angeles, California. "It was one Christmas morning in the late 1980s that I really began to turn to Anthony."

John Paul visited a close friend and his son, who is John's godson. The six-year-old boy lost his cousin's new play action figure in his grandmother's front hedge. As John watched him look for the action figure, the boy called out, "Dear Saint Anthony, please come down. Something's lost that must be found: bow and arrow."

Unable to decipher the little boy's words, spoken so rapidly, the boy's father translated for John. And the boy found the lost play action figure.

A Miraculous Recovery and a Chance
to Say Thank You

In 1953, Clare C. of Cincinnati, Ohio, was seventeen years old. Clare contracted an infection, her appendix burst, and peritonitis set in. "The doctors said there was not much hope for me, and a Catholic priest was called in to give me the last rites," Clare recalled.

As Clare's condition grew worse, and her temperature rose to 103 degrees, her mother—devoted to Saint Anthony—placed a Saint Anthony lily on Clare that she got from Mount Airy, a national shrine to Saint Anthony in Cincinnati. She also placed a small statue of Saint Anthony on the table next to Clare's bed. Then she began to pray, asking for Saint Anthony's help.

"After only a few days," Clare said, "my temperature started to drop, and I began my miraculous recovery."

Some seventeen years later, Clare and her husband visited Europe, and the tour was supposed to include a stop in Padua, where Saint Anthony is buried. "I looked forward to visiting Saint Anthony Basilica," Clare said, "and seeing his burial place."

As the tour bus approached Padua, the tour director announced that they would not be able to stop in Padua because they were behind schedule. Determined that she would get her wish to visit Saint Anthony's tomb to say a prayer of thanksgiving, Clare said to her husband, "We will see Padua." Then she bowed her head and said a prayer asking Saint Anthony to help.

"Five minutes later," Clare said, "the tour director announced that we would make a brief stop in Padua, after all."

Clare's husband's mouth dropped open in surprise, but she knew that it was a little miracle that Saint Anthony performed in answer to her prayer.

The Communist Secret Police Said
No to Entering the Seminary

In 1974, K. D. of Prague, Czechoslovakia, decided to become a Catholic priest. "Unfortunately," he said, "it was not possible because the communist secret police decided who could be admitted to the seminary, so I had no chance."

About that time, a Franciscan priest, Jan B., organized a clandestine seminary. So K. D. worked in the Insurance Enterprise and on Saturdays and Sundays he studied theology. In 1980, the state police raided the house where the clandestine seminary studies were held. Father B. was imprisoned, and all the students were investigated by the police.

Soon after this, under the stress of being investigated by the state police, K. D. had a nervous breakdown. "People said that no bishop would ordain me," he recalled. "I was rather depressed about it. But I finished the studies of theology and I prayed to our national patron saints as well as to Saint Anthony."

In 1993, K. D. was ordained a Catholic priest and became a chaplain in the parish of St. Anthony in Prague. Later, he published a book in his country about Saint Anthony.

Prayers for Their Children

What parent does not, from time to time at least, feel anxious about his or her children, regardless of their ages? But how often do parents take seriously the need to pray regularly for them?

Margery and Jim C. of Pittsfield, Massachusetts, are the parents of eight adult offspring, ages twenty-eight to forty. "You can imagine," Margery said, "that there is always one needing some prayers."

Margery and Jim heard about a weekly novena to Saint

Anthony held at a Catholic church in their town at 6:00 P.M. from March through June. Naturally concerned that their adult children seemed uncertain of themselves and had no interest in attending Mass regularly, husband and wife decided to attend the novena to Saint Anthony and pray for their children. They would, Margery said, "ask Saint Anthony to help our young people find God and themselves."

As Margery and Jim attended the weekly devotions to Saint Anthony they found a mutual affection for the saint, and each of their grown children, she said, "experienced some feeling from the power of prayer." Some are "still struggling with themselves," but they know that "we not only brought them into this world with God's help, but we are always there praying that they will someday enjoy the feeling of the powerful presence of God in their lives."

Jim and Margery both play golf, and they are not known as people who get pushy about religion. Still, they are active members of their Catholic parish and attend Mass regularly. Margery's informal golf group wondered if she attended the weekly devotions to Saint Anthony because she and Jim were praying for their unmarried offspring to each find a good spouse, or what? Margery replied that she was simply praying for each of her children to be happy with their choices. "These are all college educated young people who were caught up in the times of the 'ME' generation," Margery said, "and they needed help from Saint Anthony to find the real people they wanted to be deep down."

The next year, when it again came time for the annual novena to Saint Anthony, Margery's golfing friends "knew from whence we were coming." By that time a number of good things had happened to Margery and Jim's eight grown children. There had been one wedding, and two were making plans to attend the 1993 Youth Day in Colorado, to welcome Pope John Paul II to the United States and listen to his message. Another offspring planned to go to Haiti, to see first-hand the poverty and oppression of the people there. The others also showed signs that their lives were being touched by God and attended Mass more often.

"Saint Anthony not only touched my family," Margery said, "but also my friends, Catholic and non-Catholic, who realize that times have changed but Saint Anthony still helps us to find God within ourselves."

A Mother's Prayers for Her Son

It had not been a great year for Blaise Anthony, the son of Kathleen M. of Plymouth, Massachusetts. Named for Saint Anthony, he lived alone in Phoenix, Arizona, where during the previous year he was in an auto accident, lost his girl-friend, and had to work at a second job as a printer—work he disliked—because the job he enjoyed, as a radio DJ, did not bring in enough money to live on.

"I started praying a novena to Saint Anthony, my son's patron saint," Kathleen said. On the eighth day of the no-vena, Blaise called from a hospital to say that he was await-ing emergency surgery. At once, Kathleen and her husband boarded a plane for Phoenix.

By the time the couple joined their son at the hospital, it was after midnight on June 13, the feast day of Saint An-thony. What kind of an answer to prayer was this?

The reason for the surgery, Kathleen explained, was that Blaise had a cerebral hemorrhage. Instead of dying, or being seriously impaired, as often happens, he left the hospital three weeks later with no physical, emotional, or mental damage. "He was bald, skinny, and needing lengthy recuperation, but nothing that could not be healed." The doctors advised Blaise to give up the printing job.

So impressed was Blaise with the excellent care he received in the hospital—physical, emotional, and spiritual—that he decided to become a healthcare worker himself. "He is now a respiratory therapist," Kathleen said proudly. Blaise has been able to cope with the intense study involved and is happy because of the important work he does, so often involving infants and elderly people, to whom he is especially drawn.

"Never underestimate Saint Anthony," Kathleen said.

"Her Tony"

Margaret and Larry C. lived in a village twenty-two miles south of Buffalo, New York. Larry, a civil engineer, was preparing to take the exams for a professional engineering license in the state of New York. "These are very difficult," Margaret said, "and each applicant is allowed three tries after first qualifying to take the test."

Larry and Margaret had a good friend in Sister Saint Mark, the principal of a Catholic school in Buffalo. Sister Saint Mark had a relic of Saint Anthony, which she affectionately, and with a twinkle in her eye, called "my Tony." When she learned that Larry was to take the difficult exams for an engineering license, she lent him "her Tony" to take to the exams with him.

"This is a two day, open book exam," Margaret explained, "and Larry took two suitcases filled with engineering books with him on the morning of the first exam."

When Larry first looked at the exam, his mind went blank. Then he tried to calm down. He put the relic of Saint Anthony in his hand, then he picked up a book he hoped would be helpful, shut his eyes, and said a prayer to Saint Anthony. When he opened the more than five-hundred-page book, there was the solution to the first problem.

Larry passed the examinations on the first try, Margaret said, which is most unusual. He was always so thankful to God for answering his prayer to Saint Anthony.

"My dear husband died a few years ago," Margaret said, "but this story will never die."

Playing the Numbers for Saint Anthony

Mildred C. of Brooklyn, New York, gives much of her free time to raising money "in Saint Anthony's name," she said, for various charities. For several years she had been sending money to a priest friend in South Africa. "You could build a school, a hospital wing, a needed room, for less than three thousand dollars," Mildred said.

Not long ago her friend wrote that he was sad because he had to turn away "coloured" children from his hospital. The South African apartheid laws would not allow him to treat "coloured" children in the same areas as the white and black children—who also had to be kept separate from one another. The priest wanted badly to build a wing specifically for "coloured" children.

"So," Mildred explained, "I said 'HELP' to Saint Anthony."

The following Sunday, while she was attending Mass, Mildred prayed asking Saint Anthony for help for the hospital in South Africa. Suddenly, she envisioned the number 777. "I had never played the numbers in my life," she said. "But I went and asked my brother if he could bet one dollar for me on 777. He looked at me as if to say, 'You?!' "

Mildred won $250, which she sent to her priest friend in South Africa, and that was the beginning of the money he needed to build the new wing on his hospital.

"You Do It, and I'll Help"

On Saturday, January 1, 1994, Franciscan Father Alfred Boedekker died, ninety years old, at Saint Mary's Hospital in San Francisco, California. In 1950, Father Boedekker started St. Anthony's Dining Room in San Francisco's Tenderloin district to provide hot meals for the city's poor.

Mary R. of Alameda, California, who knew Father Boedekker for many years, said that the priest—who was known as "the patron saint of the Tenderloin"—always gave the credit for St. Anthony's Dining Room to the Franciscan saint it was named for. "Through hard times and harder times during five decades," said the *San Francisco Examiner*, "it has provided free meals to the needy every day of the year."

Father Boedekker once explained the origins of St. Anthony's Dining Room thus: "There was a recession and we were handing out meal tickets to the hungry. I thought we just had to do more than give out mere slips of paper."

St. Boniface Parish, where Father Boedekker was pastor, bought a site. Father Boedekker convinced union laborers to donate their time and remodel an old machine shop into a dining room. He asked local produce merchants and growers for food, and received donations from as far south as Bakersfield. St. Anthony's Dining Room even started its own farm, in Sonoma County, which to this day provides much of its food, although the dining room still depends heavily on outside contributions.

Father Boedekker gave all the credit to Saint Anthony. "Saint Anthony was quite a provider himself," he once said. "Today you would have called him a hustler. When I got the idea, I told him, 'Okay, you do it, and I'll help.'"

With no government subsidies, and with no financial help from the Catholic Church, St. Anthony's Dining Room has served more than twenty-three million meals since 1950. By 1994, the dining room was feeding some 2,100 people a day.

Father Boedekker was fond of telling the true story of a young man from Chicago, arrested in San Francisco for being drunk. Released from jail, he went to St. Anthony's Dining Room for a meal. After he had eaten, he asked, "When do we get down on our knees?"

"You don't have to here," a volunteer worker replied.

"When's the lecture?"

"There isn't any."

"What's the gimmick?"

The volunteer pointed to a Latin inscription on the wall: *Caritate Dei.*

"What does it mean?" the puzzled young man asked.

"Out of love for God."

"And," Father Boedekker would have added, "out of love for Saint Anthony."

"Often He Asked Me to Marry Him"

When Janice F. of Milford, Massachusetts, was a senior in high school in the early 1960s, she started dating Marc. "He was responsible, well liked, a hard worker, and very respectable," she said. "We dated for six years and often he asked me to marry him."

Janice was "very unsure," however. Her family did not want her to marry Marc. "What should have been an easy 'yes,'" she said, "turned out to be an agonizing 'I don't know.'"

Finally, Marc told Janice that if she couldn't give him an answer he would have to end the relationship so they both could get on with their lives. "I was very confused," Janice said. Then, she remembered Saint Anthony, whom she had learned about as a teenager from her sister and her aunt.

"Marc and I went to Mass together every Sunday," Janice recalled, "so I decided to ask him if he would make a novena with me and pray to Saint Anthony for an answer."

Marc agreed. For thirteen Tuesdays, which is how long this particular novena lasted, the couple prayed to Saint Anthony. Janice told Marc that her answer would come at the end of the novena, and on the final Tuesday, she said, "Yes."

"We were married the following year, 1967," Janice said. "We have been married for twenty-six years, and we have two wonderful children. Marc is a great husband and dad, and Saint Anthony has been a part of our lives for as many years."

Janice recalls that when she was in the hospital awaiting the birth of their first child, her mother was extremely nervous. Knowing this, Janice's aunt prayed to Saint Anthony that the baby would be born before 8:00 P.M., so Janice's mother could relax. The doctor said that the baby would not arrive until about 10:00 P.M. A little girl, Danielle, was born at 7:51 P.M., "much to my mom's relief," Janice said, "and the doctor's surprise."

When Janice's and Marc's son was born, they named him Anthony Marc.

Help Them to Have a Baby, Please

The brother and sister-in-law of Rita L. of North Babylon, New York, wanted a baby, but the outlook was bleak. Rita's sister-in-law had repeated miscarriages, and then she had to have one ovary removed. Doctors told her there was only a slight chance she could conceive.

"I kept up a novena to Saint Anthony," Rita said, "asking for this one-time miracle for my brother and his wife, knowing how they desired a child."

To Rita's delight, her sister-in-law did conceive successfully, and nine months later gave birth to a healthy baby boy. "They did not know of my novena at all," Rita commented.

Rita's brother's name is Anthony, but he had talked of naming the baby Frank after his and Rita's deceased father. "But while laying in her hospital bed," Rita explained, "my sister-in-law decided on Anthony."

Today, Anthony is a commercial airline pilot.

"He Lost So Much Weight That People Would Stare"

When the two sons of Mrs. Harold M. of Titusville, Florida, were three and five years old, they had to have their tonsils removed. The three-year-old bounced right back after the surgery, Mrs. M. said, but Kevin, the five-year-old, continued to languish.

"His throat hurt him, and he refused to eat. He slept most of the time," Mrs. M. said. "Finally, he didn't even want to walk."

Kevin lost so much weight that people would stare and point at him. The doctor said the boy was "doing it himself," and there was nothing wrong with him. This went on for six weeks.

"I prayed to Saint Anthony every day," Mrs. M. said, "believing he would help me."

A friend called and invited Mrs. M. and her husband to a church dinner and dance. She didn't want to go because she was so concerned about Kevin, but finally she agreed it might do her good to get out.

"We went," Mrs. M. said, "and I told my story to the woman sitting next to me. She said her son had the same experience, only he was thirteen years old when it happened." Later, Mrs. M. learned that her son was allergic to the drug used to "put him to sleep" while his tonsils were removed.

"The beautiful lady sitting next to me told me what to do when the doctor could not," Mrs. M. explained. Even though it was November and cold, Mrs. M. put Kevin outside in the fresh air, bundled up warmly. Her aunt arrived with a vanilla frosted drink, and that started Kevin back on the road to good health.

"I know it was Saint Anthony who sat me next to a stranger who helped me," Mrs. M. said.

Kevin is now an attorney in Titusville, Florida.

"Richard Was So Sick..."

Brother Bernard K. of Oakdale, New York, recalls that when Richard S. was five years old, he was so sick he had to be fed, washed, and dressed by his mother and a helper, Mrs. R.

One day in June, Richard's father, Michael, said a prayer at the end of a novena to Saint Anthony asking for Richard's recovery. All the people were given a small piece of blessed bread to take home, called Saint Anthony's bread. Michael brought his piece of Saint Anthony's bread home to his son.

"As Mr. S. was about to put the bread in Richard's mouth," Brother Bernard said, "the boy took it and exclaimed, 'I'm tired of sitting in this chair, let me get up and walk around.'" The boy quickly recovered and grew up with no ill effects from his sickness.

Untangle Those Beads!

Louise P. of Cos Cob, Connecticut, had not been a particular devotee of Saint Anthony until one day when a "knotty" problem developed. Louise has a rosary from Jerusalem, a treasured souvenir intricately designed to never get tangled. Unfortunately, the rosary did become "hopelessly tangled," she said.

"Nothing worked. Suddenly—I don't know why—I said, 'Saint Anthony, please help.'"

For a week, Louise "coaxed and pleaded" with Saint Anthony to help her get the tangles out of her rosary. Finally, annoyed, she said, "Okay, don't do it for me, do it for our Blessed Mother!"

The next morning, Louise's rosary beads were completely untangled and have remained so ever since.

"Please Help Us Find Bishop Sheen!"

On a hot Sunday afternoon in July in the early 1950s, Margaret M. of North Canton, Ohio, drove toward Youngstown, Ohio, with her mother and sister. As they drove along, Margaret remembered reading that the famous Bishop Fulton J. Sheen was going to be in Youngstown that day, and that he would be saying an outdoor Mass at one of the parish churches there.

"All three of us liked Bishop Sheen and wanted to go to the Mass," Margaret said, "but we had no idea how to find him."

As the three women continued on their way, they happened to pass a monastery in Canfield, Ohio. Margaret spotted a statue of Saint Anthony near the monastery and said, "Oh, there's Saint Anthony! Saint Anthony, please help us find Bishop Sheen."

The words were no more out of Margaret's mouth when a car full of Catholic priests pulled out of the driveway of the monastery and drove up the street ahead of her car.

"Oh boy!" Margaret exclaimed. "I'm going to follow those guys!"

Margaret's mother said, "Maybe they are going somewhere else!"

"No way. They are going to lead us to Bishop Sheen," Margaret replied.

"I stayed right behind them," Margaret said. "It wasn't easy because they were traveling fast, and traffic was heavy that afternoon. But every time they cut around a car, I cut around, too, and whenever they turned a corner, I turned also."

Finally, the priests' car turned into an alley, and Margaret followed. Suddenly, a police squad car appeared and pulled Margaret over, its lights flashing. The police officer walked up to Margaret's open window and said, "I'm sorry, but you can't come in here."

"Why?" Margaret asked. "Is this where Bishop Sheen is going to be?"

"Yes, but this area is reserved for priests. You will have to go around the block to the general parking area."

Margaret thanked the police officer and drove around the block. Her heart sank, however, when she saw how many cars there were and the huge crowds of people. "I started to worry about my mother," she recalled, "because it was such a hot day and it was getting hotter by the minute. My mother had been in and out of hospitals a number of times and would not be able to stand for very long."

The three women followed the crowd as it moved along. Soon they found themselves in an area that looked like an athletic field. But there was only one small area where there was any shade, and that was where the altar was set up. There were folding chairs everyplace, but Margaret couldn't see a single one that was empty.

"I began to pray to Saint Anthony," Margaret said. "You got us this far," she prayed, "please help us now."

Just then Margaret noticed a man on the other side of the field waving his arm. But Margaret didn't know who he was or who he was waving at. "There were people everywhere."

Soon, however, the man came jogging toward Margaret and her mother and sister. Under his arm he carried three folding chairs. "Follow me!" he said. So the three women followed the man. "He led us right down to the altar," Margaret said, "and set up the chairs right in front of the altar in the shade!"

Just as they got themselves settled, a procession of priests, with Bishop Sheen bringing up the rear, came around the corner of a building, over to the altar area, and the Mass began.

"My faith in Saint Anthony is still very much alive," Margaret said.

"I Needed a Job Badly"

Early in 1962, Donald S. of Forest Hills, New York, found himself in very difficult circumstances. His wife had just given birth to their second son a few months before, and he was without a job.

Donald's prior work experience was as an editor of manuscripts for publishing companies, but the city he and his family lived in offered few opportunities in publishing. One day followed another with no job prospects on the horizon, until about five months had gone by. "I became quite anxious and depressed," Donald said. "With a wife and two children, I needed a job badly, but I couldn't find one despite numerous efforts."

Naturally, Donald had been praying daily during this trying time, but finally, he said, "I decided I needed to make a special spiritual push, so I began a novena to Saint Anthony."

On the ninth day of the novena, Donald received an offer for a job in New York City, his hometown and a major publishing center. Donald's wife had reservations about the job, but after considering the offer for several days he accepted. "I kept the job for twenty-six-and-a-half years, until my retirement," he commented. "It turned out that Saint Anthony had selected a job that would keep me, my wife, and, as it developed, our three children in modest comfort for quite a long time."

Donald said that to him finding this job "was not just one of life's little accidents." On the contrary, "it seems quite clear to me that heaven [interceded] for me through…Saint Anthony, who has been described as 'a saint who delivers.'"

"I Came Down With Cancer"

In the middle of September 1992, Joy W. "came down with cancer." A resident of San Francisco, California, Joy "had all the tests known to man, and maybe a few more, and sure enough my left lung had to come out."

The surgery went smoothly, then a week later the doctor decided that Joy should receive radiation therapy. Joy accepted his judgment and submitted to the therapy. Near the middle of the third week of radiation, however, Joy fell three times. Attributing her falls to side-effects of radiation, she decided to discontinue the treatments.

"My internist called and wanted to know what was going on," Joy said. "He then told me he wanted a brain scan."

The cancer had spread to Joy's brain, so she began an even more intense regimen of radiation therapy over a period of about six days. By now it was the latter part of March 1993.

"All the time I was praying to Saint Anthony," Joy said. "I feel fine, no pain whatsoever. I talk to 'Tony' as I go around the house. Although I may not be cured, I am well and am in no pain. If this is a special grace, I have it through Saint Anthony."

"Poor, Dear Saint Anthony"

"In our living room, when I was a child," said Mary S. of Dearborn Heights, Michigan, "we had a large picture of Saint Anthony in an ornate, gold-gilded frame." Mary's grandmother always referred to the saint as "poor, dear Saint Anthony." This was the origin of Mary's devotion to Saint Anthony.

Many years later, circumstances made it necessary for Mary to search for an apartment. She had never lived alone before, so this was a strange, entirely new experience. Mary desperately prayed to Saint Anthony asking him to help her find a place to live. "I promised that if he did help me locate a place where I would be safe and content, I would purchase a statue and burn a vigil light in front of it as long as I lived there."

The first and only apartment Mary looked at turned out to be exactly the place for her. "I firmly believe that it was Saint Anthony's guidance that brought me to this small apartment. It was perfect. The warm and caring managers seemed to adopt all the tenants as their own, and all were well taken care of. Everyone knew everyone else, and I had a good feeling of security."

That apartment was Mary's "happy home" for thirteen

years. "Saint Anthony got his statue and his vigil light and my enduring and sincere gratitude," Mary said. And she became a more prayerful person as a result.

"My Little Brother, Nine Years Old, Was Dying"

Jennie M. of Elmont, New York, said: "Many years ago, my little brother, nine years old, was dying. I asked Saint Anthony to pray for him to be well, and I promised to always light candles for him."

Jennie was twelve years old at the time. "My brother woke up," she said, "and said he had a dream in which Saint Anthony told him to come and play with him. I knew that Saint Anthony had answered me through my brother, and he was taking him to heaven. The next day, my brother died."

Part II

SAINT JUDE
THADDEUS

*Patron of
Hopeless Situations*

"I Held the Saint Jude Medal in My Hand and Began to Pray"

Vincent S. of Howard Beach, New York, made his living during the 1950s as a traveling sales engineer for a company that produced molded rubber products. His job was to service existing customers and develop new customers and products.

One day, as he was about to depart on a sales trip, Vincent received in the mail some literature from a Saint Jude shrine in Detroit, Michigan, including a small medal of Saint Jude. "I was in a hurry," he said, "so I put the medal in my jacket pocket and took off."

On the route Vincent took that week was a large company in Bridgeport, Connecticut, that he had called on for several years without making a single sale. He decided to make a quick stop there all the same, and then head for Boston, Massachusetts. "The purchasing agent was his usual pleasant self," Vincent recalled, "but he seemed deep in thought, and I was shocked when he said, 'You know, I think we might be able to do something.' Then he was quiet again."

While the purchasing agent thought, Vincent put his hand in his jacket pocket and felt the Saint Jude medal, which he had forgotten about. "I held it in my hand," he said, "and began to pray."

Finally, the man said, "Give me a little time. Can you stop back again this afternoon?"

A few hours later, Vincent returned to the purchasing agent's office and walked out again with a purchase order for three molds which, he said, "at that time cost about five thousand dollars each." These molds would be used continuously to produce parts for the Bridgeport company. Later, the same man ordered more molds. "This customer became my largest account," Vincent said, "with sales of about one and a half million dollars per year. From that day on, I wore a Saint Jude medal and do to this day."

"The Howard Beach Merrymakers"

Vincent S., of the rubber molds story above, recalled that in his younger years when he and his wife would have "a house party," he would take out his banjo, "and we'd have a great time singing the songs of our day. My wife and I, my sister and brother-in-law, and another couple who were old-time friends hit it off pretty well, and we always enjoyed ourselves."

At this time, the group was in their late fifties. One evening, "just for the hell of it," Vincent said to his friends, "Hey, do you want to do something good before you die? We always have so much fun when we get together, why not share that fun with others? For instance, we could sing in nursing homes where they might enjoy something like this."

Everyone agreed this sounded like a great idea, so they decided to give it a shot. Vincent contacted a few nursing homes and asked if they could entertain "their guests." Nursing-home administrators were most pleased with the offer.

Because they were amateurs, Vincent and his group were a bit nervous, but they did their first "gig" on a stage in a large city-owned nursing home. "When the residents began to sing along and dance in the aisles," he said, "we gained confidence and decided to continue with our endeavor."

Naming themselves the Howard Beach Merrymakers, the group bought costumes, amplifiers, and other equipment. After several performances, they found that most of the institutions were funded for entertainment, and they insisted on paying. "However," Vincent said, "we didn't want to take any money since we felt this would take the fun out of what we originally intended to do, which was to bring joy to the elderly in nursing homes."

Because of Vincent's love for Saint Jude, he said, "Look,

we'll continue to do the gigs gratis, but if they want to pay us, we will accept it as a donation in their name to St. Jude Children's Research Hospital in Memphis, Tennessee."

Everyone agreed, and the nursing homes liked the idea, as well. Over three years and some 150 performances, the Howard Beach Merrymakers sent the hospital more than $7,000. They even got to meet entertainer Danny Thomas, who founded St. Jude's Children's Research Hospital.

In 1976, illness forced Vincent to quit both his job and the Howard Beach Merrymakers. "While in the hospital," he said, "I again called on Saint Jude, and he helped me through some major surgery and a year and a half of chemotherapy."

"Bingo, You Said the Magic Word"

Sometimes a job interview can be a strange experience. In 1978, Vincent S. of the two previous stories interviewed for a position in New York City, even though the job would be in his hometown of Howard Beach, New York. "I told the interviewer about my past experience, medical history, and so on, and during our conversation I mentioned...the Howard Beach Merrymakers and St. Jude Children's Research Hospital."

The interviewer said, "Bingo, you said the magic word—Saint Jude. You have the job."

The interviewer was a former Catholic priest. He not only gave Vincent the job but a picture of Saint Jude that he had in his wallet. "I later learned that there were twenty-eight applicants for the job," Vincent said.

"I Prayed and Prayed for a Healthy Baby Boy"

In 1970, Celina M. of Brownsville, Texas, became pregnant after giving birth to three little girls and suffering two miscarriages. "My family and I were hopeful for a healthy baby boy," she said.

Six weeks into Celina's pregnancy, a miscarriage seemed imminent. Celina's doctor instructed her to stay in bed for the next three months. "During these three months," she said, "with the help of my husband and family who helped to care for my three little girls, I prayed and prayed for a healthy baby boy. I especially prayed to Saint Jude and promised him I would name my baby boy Tadeo after Jude's second name in Spanish."

On June 16, 1971, Celina gave birth to a baby boy, "healthy and beautiful."

In 1991, Tadeo was in a terrible car accident and suffered an internal head injury. "The doctors could not give me any prognosis," Celina said, "they just said we had to wait and see."

After only one month, Tadeo was in fine condition. "I have dedicated my son to Saint Jude," Celina said, "and have asked Saint Jude to please pray for Tadeo always."

"The Specialist Told Us He Would Be Blind in Two Years"

Gloria F. of Bayside, New York, has a son who was born in the mid-1950s and has had diabetes since he was twelve years old. In 1992, Gloria said, doctors discovered that he had "severe diabetic retinopathy." An internationally recognized specialist said he would be blind in two years because there was massive bleeding behind his eyes.

Gloria's son began laser treatment, she said, "and we started novenas and daily prayers to Saint Jude."

After many treatments and two major eye operations, Gloria's son's vision began to return. "His vision is now 20-25," she said, "whereas before he could barely read the big E on the eye examination chart."

He Prayed to Saint Jude on His Brother's Behalf

James K. of Bowling Green, Ohio, has always relied on the intercession of Saint Jude to guide him through difficult times. "But," said James, "I often feel he's most powerful when my prayers are intended for someone other than myself."

James was working for the Toledo Mud Hens Baseball Club (Triple-A affiliate of the Detroit Tigers) as the team's Assistant General Manager. His identical twin brother, Tom, was waiting in the wings for *his* full-time professional sports debut.

At the time, Tom was nearing his graduation with a masters in sport administration. Throughout his anticipation, Tom actively pursued a full-time position in sports. Despite being several thousand dollars in debt, Tom remained calm for his big break. In the meantime, James prayed to Saint Jude day and night for his guidance in finding Tom a decent paying job.

"Amidst months of praying," said James, "Saint Jude came through with a roar! Pardon the pun, but my brother landed a position with the Detroit Tigers Baseball club as the team's Account Executive. Although the job pays just enough to live from paycheck to paycheck, our family is ecstatic about his success!

"Saint Jude always seems to make an impossible situation look possible."

"My Son Was Gravely Ill"

A neighbor of Gloria F. of the story above has a statue of Saint Jude on her front lawn. One day, she found a note in her mailbox. The note said, "I am a Jewish woman. My son was gravely ill. I know nothing about the statue in front of your home, who he is or what he stands for. But I stood in front of it and asked him for help. I would like you to know my son is better."

The woman did not sign her name or go into more detail than this. "But," Gloria said, "as my neighbor was telling me this I got chills and thought how wonderful Saint Jude is!…He truly is the saint of the impossible."

"At Age Fifty-Three, My Dad Lost His Job"

Monsignor John M. of Des Moines, Iowa, recalled that in the 1930s, when he was a boy, an aunt gave his parents and the five children in the family a Saint Jude prayer book. "Saint Jude became the eighth member of our household," Msgr. M. said. "All of us turned our 'impossibles' over to Saint Jude daily."

On a cold March day in 1938, the whole family shared an "impossible" that made all the others pale by comparison. "At age fifty-three," Msgr. M. said, "my dad lost his job which he held for twenty-three years. Saint Jude, 'Saint of the Impossible,' was about to get his ultimate test."

John was sixteen and about to begin, he said, his "less traveled road" of prayer. "Not that this road was untraveled, but in the next two years I traipsed it unceasingly."

Happily, Msgr. M. said, he attended a Catholic high school where he could attend daily Mass and spend a moment of prayer in the chapel during the two-minute breaks between classes. "After lunch I prayed my frayed Saint Jude prayer book and, after school, when I had a bit more time to 'chew the fat' with Saint Jude, I frayed the little book a bit more."

Money was scarce for the family, so the future Catholic priest became accustomed to the walk between home and school. "Saint Jude and I 'chewed the fat' more as we walked," he said. "On some of those walks home, I stopped into the parish church for more prayer. My day always ended in prayer as I prayed to Saint Jude for the 'impossible dream' of Dad's return to work."

Sometimes John began to doubt that Saint Jude would do anything to help find work for his father. Still, he kept praying, mainly because one of his teachers often said, "If you think you're losing your faith because you doubt, think again. Your doubts are door openers to deeper faith." So, Msgr. M. said, "I kept praying."

For two years, John's father—who had not attended high school—studied algebra, geometry, and advanced math. Finally, he took the exam for a Class A engineer's license and received a score of 96 out of a possible 100. "Twenty-four hours later," Msgr. M. said, "he applied for the position of head engineer at an aircraft factory and was hired instantly. He worked there for the rest of his seventy years."

During his two years of prayer, Msgr. M. said, he was "ticked off" at his father because he did not see him "hitting the streets" in search of a job. "Why should I pray for him if he is content with having no job?" he complained. "Little did I know that he had spent most of his time 'hitting the books' as I was 'hitting my knees.' How sheepish I felt when I discovered the truth."

While John's father worked quietly to remove his "impossible," Msgr. M. said, "Saint Jude was working quietly on one of mine."

By age eighteen, John's thoughts became filled with more than his father's need for work. He had thought of becoming a priest before, but it always seemed impossible for him. "Happily, my sessions with Saint Jude sent me inquiring about something about which I would never have prayed otherwise. Not so! Eight years later, February 21, 1948, I was ordained a priest."

From his experience of prayer to Saint Jude, Msgr. M. said, he learned much about the capacity of prayer to open the human heart to "larger realms of possibility" and about "God's longing to erase thoughts of impossibility." "Sometimes we pray for the possibility of one 'impossible' only to discover that God has in mind a far greater possibility for those who say, 'That's impossible!'"

To Adopt Another Child Seemed Impossible

"My late husband and I adopted two children," said Margaret S. of Hubbard, Ohio. The first, a girl, the couple adopted in 1953. The couple's hopes for another child, however, seemed doomed to frustration because so many couples on the waiting list had not yet adopted a first child.

On vacation in Canada in 1958, Margaret and her husband discovered that children were available for adoption there, but they would have to work through their adoption agency in the United States.

"At that time," Margaret said, "I found a booklet about Saint Jude in church and that started my devotion to him."

In 1959, a little boy in Canada became available for adoption, but the state of Ohio set up an obstacle to the adoption because the boy was judged to be "a slow learner." Although, Margaret and her husband had no problem with this and their adoption agency did all it could, the situation seemed impossible.

Finally, in 1960 another Canadian child became available for adoption. Margaret and her husband, praying frequently for Saint Jude's intercession, visited a two-and-a-half-year-old little boy in May, completed all the paperwork, and finally, in August, they were able to bring him home as their own. "So I do thank Saint Jude for our son," Margaret said.

"Our Cousin's Daughter Was Trying to Have a Baby"

In August of 1992, Sandi R. of Tacoma, Washington, became a Catholic. Her cousin's daughter Joyce and her husband John wanted to have a baby, but Joyce was unable to conceive. "Believing that new converts sometimes receive a special favor from prayer," Sandi said, "our cousin asked me to pray for her daughter."

In October, reading about a novena to Saint Jude sponsored by a Franciscan mission association, Sandi mailed her prayer request that, if it was God's will, through the intercession of Saint Jude, Joyce and John would be blessed with a child.

In August 1993, when Sandi's daughter became engaged, she sent her cousin a wedding announcement. "Our cousin called," Sandi said, "to say that she would be unable to come to the wedding because Joyce was going to have a baby! She would be eight months pregnant by then and had been having difficulties and was supposed to stay in bed. Our cousin felt she should stay close at hand just in case something went wrong."

Sandi considered this quite a miracle. "However," she said, "we were worried. Sometimes our prayers don't always turn out the way we think they should. Again, prayers to Saint Jude."

On September 22, 1993, Eric Michael was born. "A nine pound, nine ounce, perfect little baby boy."

"I will always believe," Sandi said, "that it was thanks to many prayers to Saint Jude that Joyce and John were blessed with a beautiful and healthy baby boy."

They Had to Cut Loose Their Living Room

In 1978, one of the heaviest rain seasons in recorded history pounded Los Angeles. A landslide developed where the home of John Paul A. and his parents was located. The living room had to be cut loose from the rest of the house, and down it crashed into the abyss.

"If the land movement progressed," John Paul said, "the next cut would run the length of the house, including the kitchen, the furnace, and the bedrooms."

John Paul said that during this time Saint Jude was his constant companion. "I was praying novenas to him every nine hours, let alone every nine days."

The second cut was never required. "I know Saint Jude was at work," John Paul said.

"I Ask Saint Jude for a Parking Place"

Agnes A. of Richmond Hill, New York, said that she is "a senior citizen, but I still manage to drive my own car." Once she gets to where she's going, however, Agnes finds that walking very far can be a problem. If there is no parking space near the place she wants to go, Agnes asks Saint Jude to find one for her.

"It is really something to experience," Agnes said. "If there doesn't happen to be a place in front of the store, then after a few seconds someone comes out and pulls away, and there I am."

Agnes said that her grandchildren, ages sixteen to thirty years, if they are at a shopping mall and cannot find a parking space, will say, "If Grandma was here she would ask Saint Jude."

"If I am with my sister," Agnes said, "she just looks at me and says, 'Did you?' Sometimes I have not, but most times I have."

Her Brother Bill's Drinking Problem

Sister Kathryn L. of Denver, Colorado, said that she returned both "sad and glad" from the funeral of her brother Bill. She was sad for the loss to herself and the rest of her family and her brother's friends, but glad for the memories his passing left them all. "Prayers were offered, sympathies expressed, family and friends shared memories. There was a renewed recognition of Bill's goodness, the fruit of adversity accepted and overcome."

Among the brighter events in Bill's life, Sister Kathryn said, was "the mastery of a drinking problem which gained for him lasting and deep respect, and the love of a faithful wife and family plus many friends."

"I remembered many years of daily prayers to Saint Jude," Sister Kathryn said, "for my brother Bill's drinking problem. It worked. That daily prayer did."

When Bill's status as a recovering alcoholic seemed firmly established, Sister Kathryn's prayers "switched," she said, "to thanksgiving and a greater personal love of Jesus, whose image is on the 'badge' over Jude's heart." In pictures and images of Jude, he wears a large medallion on a chain around his neck, and on the medallion is a profile image of Jesus.

Saint Jude Kept Watch Over Her Mother

Peggy O. of Rosamond, California, called upon the intercession of Saint Jude for the welfare of her mother, Dolores, when she had open-heart surgery (a double bypass) on September 19, 1992.

"We were told that although this is major surgery, it is fairly routine for the doctors involved," Peggy said. But following the surgery, Dolores went into ventricular fibrillation (a "code blue") and almost died. When the family was finally allowed to see her, my father said, "It'll be a miracle if she pulls out of this."

The next day Peggy brought a Saint Jude card into her mother's hospital room and pinned it to the bulletin board facing the bed—"to keep an eye on her when we couldn't be there," Peggy explained.

The story goes on. Dolores struggled to get better and ten days later stopped breathing—her lungs were clogged due to pneumonia. The next day, however, she was much better and was released from the hospital after thirty-three days.

Just one year and seven months after the operation,

Dolores was doing over an hour a day on her treadmill and exercised routinely. She lost almost forty pounds and, as Penny tells it, "she looks amazing. I thank God and especially Saint Jude for her recovery, for it truly looked like a 'hopeless and difficult case.'

"As for that holy card: it is now framed on the wall of her room and facing her bed, still keeping an eye on her."

"Bankruptcy Was the Ultimate Failure"

In the early morning hours of May 1, 1966, Ursula L. lay awake, certain that she was on the verge of bankruptcy. "I grew up," said the Warren, Ohio, woman, "with the belief that bankruptcy was the ultimate failure."

Ursula prayed to Saint Jude, asking his intercession. "I promised Saint Jude that I—a junk-food junkie—wold not eat or drink anything that remotely resembled junk food for five years if I did not have to file for bankruptcy."

Almost immediately after this prayer, Ursula fell into a restful sleep, and when she awoke she began to fulfill her promise to Saint Jude.

On the first anniversary of her promise, Ursula's financial situation had not improved, but she was not bankrupt, either. Still, she said, "I almost had resigned myself to the 'fact' that my prayer was not being answered."

That evening, Ursula won a $1,700 bingo door prize, which was enough to get caught up on all the bills and to plan a way out of her dire financial situation. She also kept her promise to avoid junk foods for five years.

"I learned over the years," Ursula said, "that bankruptcy for some people is a solution, not a personal failure."

"I Prayed to Saint Jude to Help Me Win"

"My son is a recovering alcoholic," said Ursula, of the story just before this one. "He is also proud of his Irish heritage."

So proud is Ursula's son of being Irish that he made a leprechaun suit complete with shiny buckles on the shoes. On Saint Patrick's Day, he and a group of his friends from Alcoholics Anonymous go to a bar and try to set an example of a way to have fun without drinking alcoholic beverages.

"I wanted to be able to be a part of this just one time," Ursula said, "but I knew I could not afford the trip to San Diego, where he lives."

In September 1989, the company Ursula works for sponsored a contest. Three people would win trips to a company convention in San Diego the week of March 13. "I began praying to Saint Jude to help me win one of the three trips. One of the contests had to do with years of service, and I thought I would win one for sure."

Unfortunately, Ursula did not win one of the three trips to San Diego. About this time, a friend told Ursula that she and her husband wanted to buy a house, but she was worried that they would not qualify for a loan. "I told her to pray to Saint Jude, and he would take care of things. She was very skeptical, but she started to pray to Saint Jude."

Ursula admitted to her friend that she had prayed to Saint Jude to win a trip to San Diego but she had not won. "I told her not to let that discourage her, however, because I was sure that there was a good reason for not having my prayers answered to win the contest."

The week before the convention in San Diego, Ursula's boss called her into his office. He told her that since she had tried so hard to win the contest, and because she would have won a trip except for an oversight on his part, he would send her to the convention after all.

"When my friend found out I was going to California," Ursula said, "she began praying even harder and with less skepticism. When I got home from California she greeted me with the news that she and her husband had gotten their house."

"He Drove My Mother Crazy"

Robert L. of Fort Wayne, Indiana, said that his older brother was "one of those who could never quite get a career going." Although he was a college graduate, it looked like he might be a bank teller for the rest of his life. "He drove my mother crazy," Robert said.

Eventually, Robert's brother even lost his job as a bank teller which, Robert said, "forced my mother to [make] a novena to Saint Jude."

Robert's mother had already had a "Thank you, Saint Jude" notice printed in a newspaper when her older son landed a new and better job. "She told me," Robert said, "that she always had her 'thank you' notice printed right away because she knew Saint Jude had answered her prayer one way or another.

"The upshot," Robert said, "was the encounter with my brother. When he came to tell my mother of his new job, she informed him that he owed it all to Saint Jude. My brother was not amused: 'Mom, he's the patron saint of hopeless causes!' Her response: 'Exactly.'"

"The Baby Would Be Retarded and Have Spina Bifida"

Five months into her first pregnancy, Janet S. of Niles, Ohio, went to have a routine sonogram, which would result in an x-ray-like image of the developing baby. A week later, Janet's doctor asked her to have another sonogram because the first one seemed to show a problem with the baby's spine.

"My husband and I were told that the baby had a fracture near the tip of the spine," Janet said. "We were told that this was very severe and that the baby would probably be retarded and have spina bifida."

Janet and her husband had an appointment with a fetal specialist. They were told that "if" they went through with the pregnancy they should seek counseling to learn how to deal with a handicapped baby.

"As a Catholic," Janet said, "there was no question in my mind but to go with the gift that God had given us."

Janet and her husband had to wait two more weeks before another sonogram could be done. Janet's mother gave her a candle to light while they prayed a nine-day novena to Saint Jude. "My whole family and our friends joined us in saying every prayer we could think of." They also prayed to Saint Gerard, the patron saint of mothers.

After two weeks, the next sonogram was done by the fetal specialist. "We were told that everything was fine," Janet said. "The spine no longer showed a fracture. A miracle? Yes, we believe so."

The doctor showed Janet and her husband the films from the first and last sonograms, and they could see the baby's spine with and without the fracture.

Janet began labor on Christmas day 1988, and gave birth to a healthy baby girl by Caesarean section the next day.

"We feel that our faith in God and in our saints did help to heal our baby's spine."

"She Was Diagnosed With Ulcerative Colitis"

In August of 1988, the eleven-year-old granddaughter of Mrs. William M. of Brooklyn, New York, was on a camping trip in California with her parents and some friends. She began to complain of stomach pains. After a visit to a doctor's office, she was diagnosed with ulcerative colitis.

Mrs. M.'s granddaughter was hospitalized for one month, receiving nutrition only through a tube in her arm. She received seven blood transfusions and had a fever of 105 degrees. Mrs. M. stayed with the other children while the girl's mother stayed at the hospital day and night.

Finally, the doctors decided that only surgery could solve the problem. All along, Mrs. M. said, "Saint Jude was besieged with prayers and novenas."

"Today," Mrs. M. said, "she's doing great. She plays sports and is looking forward to high-school graduation. This is only one of Saint Jude's miraculous wonders."

"The Baby Was in a Breech Position"

In 1947, Jane G. of Springfield, Illinois, was pregnant with her and her husband's third child. The due date had passed, and the doctor determined that the baby was in a breech position. "Sister Mary Aquinas, a Franciscan friend, suggested we make a novena to Saint Jude," Jane said. "We did, and on October 28, Saint Jude's feast day, the baby turned himself to the proper position and was born within a few hours."

"I Was Drafted Into the Army"

In 1967, nineteen-year-old Craig G. of Duquesne, Pennsylvania, received notice that he was being drafted into the U.S. Army, and he had two weeks before he was to report for induction. "I worked in a steel mill," Craig said, "so I took the second week for my vacation and did what I wanted to do, play sandlot baseball."

While Craig enjoyed playing baseball, he also prayed to Saint Jude to help him not be drafted. As the induction date drew near, however, his prayers seemed to go unanswered. Then, one day while playing in the outfield Craig went back for a fly ball, and his knee gave out. He collapsed to the ground in pain. Pulling himself to his feet, he continued to play until the next inning when his knee buckled again, forcing him to leave the game.

Craig reported for duty in the army, but while he was in basic training he was checked by an orthopedic physician who reclassified him from 1-A to 1-Y. Craig received a medical discharge. "I did not have to stay in the army nor go to Vietnam," Craig said. "Saint Jude had answered my prayer."

Craig said that at the time, he believed that Saint Jude had worked a miracle for him. But as his faith developed later in life he realized that the source of his "miracle" was God, while Saint Jude was the intermediary.

"Saint Jude Has Answered Many of My Requests"

It's difficult for Mary W. of Fairborn, Ohio, to narrow down her list of the ways she has been helped by the prayers of Saint Jude. "I feel like over the years Saint Jude has answered so many of my requests," she said.

Tops on her list is her husband's survival of a drinking problem. "For many years," she said, "my husband would drink too much and drive [afterward]. I prayed to Saint Jude that my husband would make it home, and he always did. Today he has full control of his drinking, he knows when to stop, and he never drives when drinking."

One time, Mary said, she and her husband owed about $18,000 to a credit union. "I prayed to Saint Jude that we could pay it off in a hurry." With Saint Jude's help, Mary said, they paid off the loan in six years.

Mary also has a grown son who is a recovering alcoholic. "I thought he would never come around," she said, "and he was even on drugs." Mary prayed often to Saint Jude, asking his help for her son.

"Finally, one day he woke up and decided to turn his life around. Now he goes to Alcoholics Anonymous meetings often, and it has been three years. Now he thinks it is stupid to drink. Thanks again to Saint Jude."

"X-Rays Showed a Bacterial Infection"

In 1990, Eleanor G. of Tonawanda, New York, was on her way to attend Mass at her parish church. An accident occurred in the church parking lot. "People banged into me and knocked me down, and my hip was broken," she said. "One couple saw me and rushed to me."

As a result of the mishap, Eleanor had to undergo a hip replacement. Then, in September 1993, she learned that she had a "micro-movement" in her hip where the replacement was done. "X-rays showed a bacterial infection had caused this," she explained.

Eleanor prayed regularly to Saint Jude while under her doctor's care. By January 1994, the micro-movement disappeared, and the infection with it. For Eleanor, her recovery was "a miracle."

"The Doctors Had Difficulty Identifying the Type of Cancer"

In August 1988, said Patricia C. of Brooklyn, New York, a visit to her doctor's office resulted in an x-ray that showed a "mass" in her chest cavity. Further investigation confirmed that Patricia had lymphoma. However, she said, "the doctors were having great difficulty trying to identify the type of cancer." Finally, tissue samples were sent to the Sloan-Kettering Cancer Center.

A friend who learned of Patricia's situation sent her a relic of Saint Jude. "At this point," Patricia said, "I asked Saint Jude to 'put his finger on the slides' to help the doctors make a determination so that we could start treatment."

On September 17, the Sloan-Kettering report arrived stating that Patricia had "B-cell lymphoma with T-cell involvement." Four days later, Patricia underwent the first of five chemotherapy treatments she would have between then and December 16.

"Whenever I was hospitalized," Patricia said, "I brought a small statue of Saint Jude and placed it on my night table. I said my novena prayers and rosary daily. Being presumptuous, I really never had any doubt that I would get better."

As of January 1994, Patricia had been in remission for five years.

"Although my head tells me that my outstanding medical treatment helped me get better," Patricia said, "my heart knows that Saint Jude told the doctors what I had and then helped me get well."

"The Car Would Not Start"

"Saint Jude has been a great intercessor for our family," said Donna G. of Buffalo, New York.

Years ago, on a "terribly cold Sunday morning," when Donna was a ten-year-old in Nebraska, the family prepared to leave for Mass. "Our family *never* missed Mass," Donna said.

But the car would not start, and neither would the truck. "Dad came back in the house with this [distressing] news," Donna said. "Our mother said, 'Take the three older children, and Saint Jude will start the truck.'"

Donna's father, a convert to Catholicism, "just had a time being convinced of this," but finally he did as his wife instructed.

"The truck started right up," Donna said. "So some of the family, at least, was able to attend Mass."

"My Son Found Out He Was HIV-Positive"

"I have a son," said Celia S., "who is a recovered drug addict. My husband and I went through four years of hell with his addiction."

Finally, the Brooklyn, New York, woman said, her prayers to Saint Jude were answered. Her son entered and completed a drug-rehabilitation program. Later, he finished a master's degree and passed a course to become a certified public accountant. "Today," Celia said, "he is a CPA for a large company. He met a lovely girl and got married."

A year later, Celia's son's wife become pregnant. "It should have been a happy occasion for us, but my son also found out he is HIV-positive." The family was worried that the baby would also be infected, but, Celia said, her prayers to Saint Jude and Saint Anthony were answered. "Gabriella was born on the feast of the Ascension, May 24, 1990, and she is healthy."

Celia said that her son's health has been good. "He goes for a checkup every month. His T-cells are up in the 500 range, which is not too bad. His wife thinks it is her cooking that is keeping him well, but I know it is the prayers of Saint Jude and Saint Anthony that are doing it. I don't know what the future will bring, but I will put all my trust in Jesus."

"Their House Sold the First Day It Was on the Market"

In November 1993, Robert and Irene W. moved from San Ramon, California, to a new home in Lake Oswego, Oregon. Their daughter and son-in-law wanted to join them, but first they had to sell their home in California.

"I prayed to Saint Jude," Irene said, "for our daughter and son-in-law to sell their home in San Ramon quickly so they could buy one they had just seen in Lake Oswego when visiting. The house sold the first day it was on the market! With the marvel of fax machines, they were able to buy their house in Oregon the same day."

"An Eye Surgeon Diagnosed My Condition As EALS Disease"

In 1953, Frederick W. of Ocean City, New Jersey, had a vitreous hemorrhage in his left eye. "I went to an eye surgeon," he said, "who diagnosed my condition as EALS disease."

The eye surgeon injected cortisone into Frederick's eye and told him there was no cure for this condition. Frederick became blind in his left eye for about six months and had repeated injections for over a year until finally no further injections were possible. The doctor told Frederick that he would most likely lose all vision in his other eye, as well.

The eye surgeon sent Frederick to the Shea Eye Institute and to four other eye surgeons for evaluation. None of the other doctors offered him any hope. Frederick's doctor gave him a maximum of ten years before he would be completely blind.

"I mentioned my condition to the Franciscan Sisters in our parish," Frederick said, "and one of the nuns sent to Italy for a relic of Saint Jude. I prayed to him and applied the relic to my eyes every morning and evening for God's help, and after six months I was able to see some improvement."

Frederick's doctor was amazed that he was able to see again. "He was a Jewish doctor, and he told me I must have had help from someone up above, as he could not have restored my sight."

Frederick still has some of the effects of the hemorrhage in his left eye, but with glasses he has 20-20 vision. "I still prayerfully use the relic every morning and night and thank God and Saint Jude for his intercession and for helping me in my situation. I know it was Saint Jude who interceded for me with our Lord and answered my prayers."

"I Desperately Needed a House for Myself and My Two Children"

In the mid 1950s, Rose Eileen J. of Santa Cruz, California, accepted a teaching position in a Catholic elementary school in Menlo Park, California. "I desperately needed a house for myself and my two children," she said.

Rose Eileen's sister and mother—who had suffered a stroke—wanted to move from Santa Barbara and join Rose Eileen and her children. "The father of one of my pupils worked in real estate, and he told me to go look at a house in a good location. I was saying a three-day novena to Saint Jude, and I bought the house. After three days all negotiations were completed."

"Dear Old God Must Have Laughed in Delight"

In her student nursing days, Norene P. of Verdigre, Nebraska, was disappointed when she and one of her suitors began to drift apart. She liked this guy! At this time, Norene said, "Saint Jude got a workout."

Norene prayed to Saint Jude. "Did it work?" she asked. "Yes. But not in the way I expected when I dutifully knelt in prayer. Dear old God must have laughed in delight because He knew there were other directions my life would go, and He surely must have told Jude that 'not now but someday you'll get your credit.'"

If Norene had married "that man of my dreams," she said, she would have been widowed more than ten years ago. "And I wouldn't have ended up with the guy I did and the five particular kids that I did, all of whom proved beyond any doubt that my young wishes were not best."

Of course, Norene commented, she will never know what her life would have been like had her prayers been answered as she wanted them to be answered at the time. "But there are so many times every week that I am grateful for life as it is right now."

The Bank Was About to Foreclose

"My husband died in 1966," said Mary E. of Spokane, Washington. "A few weeks after his death I got a call from the bank informing me that if I did not come up with the past-due mortgage payments on a certain piece of property, they would begin foreclosure proceedings within three days."

Mary knew that she could not make those payments. Her husband's battle with cancer had wiped out their assets. "My only income was Social Security, and I had a young son to raise."

Mary sat at her kitchen table. "No time for a novena. I simply cried out: 'Saint Jude, this is your department. HELP!'"

That afternoon, Mary went to her attorney's office to take care of some business related to her husband's estate. In the waiting room, she met "a fine Catholic gentleman" from her parish, the owner of a plumbing business.

"In our conversation," Mary recalled, "I told him of my dilemma. He suggested I give him the key so he could go look at the house."

Later, after inspecting the house, the man told Mary, "You're lucky that the house is empty. That floor in the bathroom is dangerous. If you were in the tub you might find yourself in the basement."

The man asked Mary, "What do you want for your equity?" She replied, "I need a washing machine. Two hundred dollars will do it."

The man bought the house from Mary, making all the back mortgage payments. He rebuilt the bathroom and installed new plumbing. "It became a good rental investment for him," Mary said, "and a big load off my shoulders. Saint Jude was really 'on the ball.'"

"Dad Was Without a Job in the Depths of the Great Depression"

In 1932, John P. of Sweetgrass, Montana, lived in Hamilton, Montana, with his parents and four brothers and sisters, ages three to ten. John's father was chief of police. That year, the family moved to Portland, Oregon, where John's father worked for the United States Treasury Department, helping to enforce the Alcohol Prohibition Act. "Elliot Ness stuff," John explained.

In 1934, Prohibition was repealed. "Dad and all his co-workers were left without a job in the depths of the Great Depression," John recalled.

All efforts to find another job were unsuccessful. "Mother's cousin Ethel," John said, "was living in Portland with her parents at that time, and she suggested to Mother that she make a novena to Saint Jude, the patron of impossible problems."

John's mother had never heard of Saint Jude, even though she grew up in an Irish Catholic family in Butte, Montana. All the same, John said, "we certainly made the novena."

Taking pen in hand, John's father wrote a letter to Montana state senator Burton K. Wheeler explaining his situation. Even though he achieved the highest scores in tests for government jobs, he was bumped in favor of native Oregonians when the jobs were handed out.

In the end, however, "Saint Jude came through," John said. "Dad received an appointment as officer in charge of U.S. Immigration in Havre, Montana."

When John's Aunt Ethel—who suggested the novena to Saint Jude—heard the news, she informed John's mother that the Catholic parish in Havre was named Saint Jude's Parish. "We were soon on our way back to Montana," John said.

"I Told Her to Stay With Him While I Asked Saint Jude for a Miracle"

In 1986, Maureen B. of Temple, Texas, lived in La Habra, California. Each day she attended Mass at the chapel in St. Jude Hospital in Fullerton, California.

"My neighbor Martha was considering getting a divorce," Maureen recalled, "because she had been married twenty years and never conceived a child."

Martha loved her husband Tony, but she wanted to have a child before she was too old.

"I told her to stay with Tony for one [more] year," Maureen said, "while I asked Saint Jude for a miracle."

In February 1987, Martha gave birth to a beautiful baby girl. "She is still married to Tony," Maureen said. "I never said a novena or any special prayers. I just asked Saint Jude to please ask God to send Martha and Tony a baby."

"For Four Years We Tried to Conceive a Child"

Carol S. teaches in a Catholic school in Seattle, Washington. "My husband and I tried for four years to conceive our second child," she said. "I have always been a Saint Jude fan, so the novenas began almost immediately."

Through three surgeries, Carol said, she kept a little medal of Saint Jude pinned to her hospital gown. "I kept making novenas to Saint Jude through four miscarriages. I knew the 'Saint of the Impossible' would come through in due time. My Nana always said, 'God is slow but sure!'"

On Valentine's Day 1991, Carol gave birth to a son. Nineteen months later, a daughter was born. "We were truly blessed," Carol said, "and I know Saint Jude had a hand in it."

Out of Gas on the Trans-Canada Highway

"Late one night we—my uncle and aunt, my mother, a cousin, and myself—were out of gas on the Trans-Canada Highway," said Jeffrey D. of Dartmouth, Nova Scotia, "outside of St. John, New Brunswick. As usual, these things always happen at inconvenient times and places."

Jeffrey quickly sent "an SOS to God and my 'pal' Saint Jude." Within fifteen minutes, a tow truck arrived from an all-night garage. "My uncle flagged him down," Jeffrey said, "and he got us into St. John and the service station."

Right across from the garage was an elegant old hotel "in the grand Victorian style—the Admiral Beatty Hotel." Jeffrey's uncle explained to the hotel clerk about their predicament. "He put us up in the Royal Suite for the night at a nominal charge," Jeffrey said. "To say the least, I was flabbergasted at the spectacular answers to prayer on the part of Saint Jude."

"They Tried Many Routes to Adopt a Child"

"My daughter and her husband had been married for several years," said Vivian E. of Williamsport, Pennsylvania, "and had tried unsuccessfully to conceive a child."

After surgeries and testing proved ineffective, the couple decided to adopt. "However, adoption of an infant is most difficult because of the large number of abortions and young women who keep their children even if they are not married," Vivian said. "They tried many routes to try to adopt a child, and after eight years they were finally successful through a Catholic agency."

During all this time, Vivian said, she prayed to Saint Jude to intercede with God that her daughter and son-in-law might have the joy of raising a child. "I believe they were given this child because of the intercession of Saint Jude."

"I Developed an Arthritic Condition in Both My Knees"

Robert C. of Forest Hills, New York, has been a church organist since he was seven years old. In 1973, however, he decided to seek further employment in the business community, and eventually he found a position with a Wall Street firm. "I still played the organ," he said, "and I never lost my love of God or for the Church."

Later in life, Robert said, "I developed an arthritic condition in both my knees. This made simple walking and the use of public transit virtually impossible."

Finally, in April 1990, his condition had deteriorated so much that he was forced to take an early retirement. "It wasn't too long afterward," he said, "that I got so fed up with everything that I was ready to give up, in every way and everything. Most of my so-called friends were too busy to call…I wasn't able to go anywhere. [And] money was getting a little tight."

Robert happened to find an old prayer to Saint Jude, which he began to say every day. "My health hadn't improved. If anything it had [deteriorated], but my outlook toward the future improved greatly. I know Saint Jude is the saint of impossible cases, and knowing this has helped me considerably. At least now he and I could face the future together."

But there is more to the story. Robert was so grateful to Saint Jude for the inspiration to keep going that in March 1991, he found it financially possible to buy a statue of Saint Jude, three feet high.

At this time, Robert read an article about how to get Social Security benefits, even though he was not old enough for the usual retirement benefits. Robert spoke with his doctor, but he said that it was very doubtful that Robert could qualify.

Robert said a prayer to Saint Jude, asking him for help. If Saint Jude came through, Robert prayed, he would give something in return. Robert contacted the Social Security office, filled out the forms they gave him, and began to pray again. By late July 1992, Robert had been directed by the Social Security Administration to have a medical examination and x-rays. In September, he received a letter. "I thought for sure that since they had responded so quickly all my endeavors were in vain."

Holding the letter, Robert looked at his statue of Saint Jude. "It was as if he were saying, 'We're in this together, have courage and a little faith. No matter what happens I'll still be with you.'"

Robert opened the letter, and not only did he read that he would get the benefits he hoped for, but the Social Security Administration would send him a check for benefits retroactive from the last day he had worked, in April 1990.

"You can't tell me," Robert said, "that Saint Jude didn't work a miracle. Many people told me that getting benefits from Social Security is almost impossible. One person even told me to have a lawyer standing by."

Robert said that his "near and dear friend had come through for me." Now how could he give something in return? He made a donation to St. Jude's Shrine in Cincinnati, Ohio, as well as to St. Jude's Children's Hospital in Memphis, Tennessee. "Saint Jude is indeed a true friend," Robert said. "He has given me a new lease on life.... Miracles are possible."

"An Adverse Reaction to Prostate Surgery"

"I've been invoking Saint Jude's aid for more years than I can recall," said retired attorney John B. of Springfield, Massachusetts. Most recently, John had reason to call on Saint Jude's help for a health problem. "I had an adverse reaction to prostate surgery in January 1992, caused by a drug I had been [taking] for three years for another condition."

Praying to Saint Jude, John traveled to Boston for a second medical opinion, followed by another surgery and further tests. "I feel I've finally turned the corner," John said. "Thank God!"

"She Had an Unplanned Pregnancy and Was Very Fearful"

Marie F. of Mamou, Louisiana, tells the story of her mother-in-law Rowena F. who gave birth to her first child during World War II. This little girl was born with a port-wine stain—a kind of birthmark—covering her face. After the war, another child was born with spina bifida and other birth defects.

"The types of birth defects Rowena's children had are related," Marie explained, "and because of other similar birth defects in her husband's family, Rowena was afraid to have other children."

However, several years later, Rowena found herself unexpectedly pregnant again. Deeply fearful, she made a novena to Saint Jude and promised to name the child after him if he or she was born healthy. She gave birth to a healthy baby boy and named him Thaddeus, for Saint Jude Thaddeus.

One year later, Rowena became pregnant again, and again she made a novena to Saint Jude, promising to name this baby for Saint Jude also, if he or she was born without defect. "His name is Timothy Jude," Marie said, "and he is my husband."

"My Doctor Said I Had Lost the Baby"

Virginia B. of Wood Ridge, New Jersey, has seven children. In the fourth month of her fourth pregnancy, Virginia was hospitalized. She had had miscarriages before, and there were danger signs this time, too. Lying in a hospital bed, she began to feel a great deal of pain, so she called for help.

A young, inexperienced nurse brought Virginia a bed pan,

then came back in a short time and took the contents away for disposal. From her description of the contents to a supervising nurse, it was concluded that Virginia had miscarried.

Very upset, that night Virginia was unable to sleep. "Suddenly," she said, "I realized there was a lady sitting in the corner of my room. I could see her clearly. She wore a white dress and a blue cape. Quietly but clearly she said, 'Do not cry. Pray to Saint Jude. Your prayers will be answered.'"

Virginia had never heard of Saint Jude before, but she did as the lady instructed. The next morning, Virginia's doctor told her that he was sorry, but she had lost the baby. "As he spoke," Virginia said, "I felt movement." Three times in quick succession she felt the fluttering movement of a child within her.

The doctor finally agreed to put his hand on Virginia's abdomen to feel what she could feel, and he did, indeed. "Explanations were many," Virginia said, "'probably a fraternal twin,' and so on."

Virginia's story does not end here, however. No one knew the lady who had told her to pray to Saint Jude. They all said she did not exist. "I wanted to thank her for introducing me to Saint Jude. How could someone who did not exist introduce me to a saint I did not know?"

Virginia's son, David Jude, was born October 25, 1951. "[A] wonderful, healthy baby," she said.

"She Suddenly Had a 'Ringing' in Her Ears"

Sister Darlyne K. of Leavenworth, Kansas, said that her mother, Mary Wells K., "had the practice of asking Saint Jude for some favor and then publishing her thanks by inserting the prayer to Saint Jude in the classified advertising section of our hometown newspaper. It cost ten dollars each time." Although Sister Darlyne told her mother that she could save money by writing instead to the St. Jude Society, she persisted in her customary practice.

When Mary was about eighty years old, she suddenly had a "ringing" sound in her ears. Her doctor told her the condition was common but that nothing could be done about it. She would just have to put up with it.

"One day," Sister Darlyne said, "I asked her how her ears were, and she said, 'I don't have that ringing anymore. Saint Jude cured it.' She spoke matter-of-factly, but I was astounded."

Three Responses From Saint Jude

In 1983, the youngest son of Mrs. J.L.D. of Ringgold, Georgia, had a pituitary tumor. Before surgery could be performed the boy had cortisone injections for one month. During this time, Mrs. D. said, she prayed to Saint Jude on her son's behalf. "He was operated on on Good Friday," she said, "and believe me I had been in 'Gethsemani' since the time he was diagnosed."

The doctor said that the tumor was the size of a tangerine, and it would take up to eight hours to completely remove it from the pituitary gland. Less than an hour after the surgery began, however, the doctor was out of the operating room with the news that the operation was over.

When the doctor incised the tumor he discovered that the blood supply to the tumor had been cut off and it had liquified. There wasn't even material to do a biopsy. "My son is still healthy to this day," Mrs. D. said.

Mrs. D.'s granddaughter was born with a hole in her heart and had difficulty breathing. "Who else would I go to but Saint Jude?" she asked.

Eleven days later, the baby was released form the hospital, completely healthy. The hole in her heart was no longer there.

A friend of Mrs. D. had a kidney transplant. Now she was in the hospital again for a possible second kidney transplant. "She is diabetic," Mrs. D. said, "and her foot was so bad they were talking of removing it." Mrs. D. prayed, asking Saint Jude's prayers for her friend.

"After thirty days in the hospital, her foot healed," Mrs. D. said, "and she went home without needing a second kidney transplant."

"For Twelve Years I Had Been Homeless"

"For twelve years I had been homeless," said Desiree J. of New York City. "Then in late 1991, I started praying and making a novena to Saint Jude. I also attended a novena to Saint Jude held at St. Francis of Assisi Church in Manhattan. I made a novena of thanksgiving to Saint Jude, even though I did not yet have what I prayed for, a place to live."

In September 1992, Desiree received a summons from the New York City Housing Authority asking her to attend a special interview. "I was given a lovely one-bedroom apartment at a quite affordable cost," she said. "Thanks to Saint Jude."

"Living in the Gutters of a California City"

Jan A. of Seattle, Washington, is a writer and speaker. She was giving a Welcome Home program in a Seattle parish for people returning to the Catholic Church.

"A man told me," Jan said, "that he was coming back to the Church because of a novena his mother [had] made to Saint Jude." Remarkably, however, she did not make the novena for this man. She made it for her other son.

"The other son," Jan said, "was a brilliant man whose life had been shattered by severe drug abuse. At the time of the novena, the guy was homeless, addicted, and literally living in the gutters of a California city."

On the last day of his mother's novena, the man suddenly

decided he was disgusted with himself and needed to go straight. So he did, as simple as that. His brother—the man Jan met—was so impressed with this miracle that he decided to return to Catholicism.

"One novena," Jan said, "and two prodigal sons reform their lives. Saint Jude suddenly had more respect in my eyes."

"My Coat Was Gone With an Old One Left in Its Place"

Now and then, it seems, Saint Jude gets a piece of Saint Anthony's action in the "lost articles" department. In 1977, Lisa F. of Indianapolis, Indiana, was in the seventh grade and living in Woodbury, Minnesota. "I was becoming an avid skier," she said, "and so my birthday present from my parents was a down-filled ski jacket costing over one hundred dollars."

Lisa wore her new coat everywhere, including to the first day of a state swim meet held several miles away from home. There were hundreds of spectators there. "Being young, naive, and trusting," she said, "I hung my coat with all the others. After several hours, we were the last to leave. My coat was gone, with an old one left in its place."

Lisa knew that she would be unable to return the next day to look for her coat, so she figured it was lost for good. Her mother was understanding and tried to comfort Lisa by telling her that, after all, it was only a coat. Lisa's parents, however, could not afford to replace it.

Had Lisa ever heard of Saint Jude, her mother wondered, the saint of "lost causes"? "We prayed together that day," Lisa said, "asking for the intercession of Saint Jude, that the jacket would be returned, even though there was no name or address anywhere on it."

The next day, some of Lisa's friends attended the second day of the swim competition. They phoned to tell Lisa that her coat had not been found, even though there had been several public announcements about it. At the end of the day, Lisa's friends called again. Her coat had been found on a hanger where the old one had been left, as good as new!

"My mother and I realized," Lisa said, "that God heard our prayers. Because of what happened, Mom decided to make a donation to the St. Jude Hospital in Memphis, Tennessee."

"I Placed My Purse on My Car Before I Got In"

On her way to work one morning, Lisa F. of the preceding story placed her purse on top of her car just before she got in. "Forgetting it was there," she said, "I drove away, losing it somewhere on the way to work, five miles away in the city."

As soon as she arrived at her destination, Lisa realized her mistake and immediately backtracked looking for her purse. It was nowhere in sight. "Not only did my purse contain money, my checkbook, my driver's license, and credit cards, but it also contained both my husband's and my birth certificates, my original Social Security card, and my only up-to-date address book."

Later that evening, Lisa called her mother, who reminded her of Saint Jude. "I knew she was going to say it," Lisa said.

Although she remembered what Saint Jude had done to find her coat years before, this time she was very skeptical. All the same, Lisa and her mother again prayed asking for Saint Jude's intercession for the return of at least the documents in Lisa's purse.

Two days passed with no word, "but," Lisa said, "the prayers continued." By the third day, Lisa had all but given up hope. Then, the morning of the third day, she received a phone call from a woman who said that her two young children had found the purse in a parking lot. Everything was in it except the money. Someone must have found the purse near where Lisa had lost it, taken the money, then dumped it in the parking lot where the woman's children found it.

After Lisa phoned her mother, "she sent me the forms to make a donation to the St. Jude Hospital. I was not raised in the Catholic faith and have little knowledge of the many different saints. But I am a Christian, and I believe that God heard my pleas through Saint Jude who interceded on my behalf."

She Found Herself at the Bottom of the Sewer Pipe

"It was October, and the sky was a pearly blue," recalled Frances H. of District Heights, Maryland. Frances's friend, Mary F., took Penny, her large brown-and-black beagle hound, out of her car to let her run on a wide expanse of green lawn on a naval base across the Potomac River from a sewage plant that served Washington, D.C. The wind was blowing the other way, so there was no problem with the unpleasant smell from the sewage plant.

Mary strolled along enjoying the serenity of the early evening, while Penny ran happily ahead. Lost in her own sense of peace and well-being, Mary did not notice right away that Penny was not at her heels. Suddenly realizing that her dog was not in sight, Mary retraced her steps. She heard canine cries from a manhole that, upon closer inspection, proved to have no cover. Penny was at the bottom of a large, dark pipe leading to the sewer. Iron bars across the bottom of the pipe had kept Penny from being swept away.

Mary leaned over and tried to reach Penny, but to no avail. Suddenly, Mary slipped and before she knew what had happened she found herself at the bottom of the large sewer pipe with Penny. It was dark and spooky down there, not to mention cold and wet. Mary reached down and lifted Penny to her shoulder to keep her safe.

"What are we going to do now, Penny?" Mary asked. She was frightened, not knowing what to do. Who would save them? Mary shouted and called without expecting anyone to hear her. She had seen no one else nearby when she began her peaceful evening walk, and the guard at the gate of the naval base was too far away to hear her.

Mary began to cry, and she prayed to Saint Jude who, she remembered, had been known to come to the aid of the helpless, and she and Penny certainly qualified. Mary hoped that her husband, Lloyd, would come looking for her. Her shoulders began to ache from the weight of the dog, and she continued her prayers to Saint Jude.

"The wind began to bluster overhead, at the other end of the pipe, enhancing the ghostly feeling of the prison shared by woman and dog," Frances said. "Mary reconciled herself to the thought that she and Penny would die together."

Mary and Penny remained at the bottom of the pipe all night, shivering and terrified. Finally, daylight came and with it the tide burst in with a rush. The water rose to Mary's armpits and tore away her slacks as it passed through. Her terror renewed, Mary screamed, but her cries went unheeded. Once again, she took up her prayers to Saint Jude.

Finally, a man walking nearby heard Mary's shouts and appeared at the top of the manhole. At first speechless when he saw a woman and a dog at the bottom of the large pipe, he yelled that he would get help right away. Mary was overjoyed, and before long an ambulance arrived from the naval base. The sailors who came to the rescue first pulled Penny out, but by the time they got Mary up to ground level again, the dog had done another disappearing act.

At the hospital, medical personnel attended to Mary and called her husband and the police, who had been searching for her all night. Mary received a mild tranquilizer and slept soundly under warm blankets, confident that Saint Jude and Lloyd would find Penny.

Lloyd had a set of keys to Mary's car, and with the help of the police he found it before long. "As they approached the car," Frances said, "there was Penny, waiting patiently."

To this day, years later, Mary always wears a medal of Saint Jude around her neck, and there is a replica of Penny in front of the fireplace in Mary's home.

"It Seemed Like the Cancer Must Have Spread"

In 1992, John E. of Stamford, Connecticut, and president of a major corporation, had surgery for prostate cancer. Following the operation to remove his prostate, doctors told John the cancer had not spread beyond the prostate itself. However, a follow-up blood test one month after the operation revealed otherwise. Still, John's doctor told him that this was normal and not to worry. A month later another test was done, and the results were not good. "It seemed like the cancer must have spread far beyond where it was initially found," John recalled.

John happened to notice a "Saint Jude's Novena" ad in the classified section of the local weekly newspaper. "The ad claimed that if I would repeat the prayer nine times a day for nine days, by the eighth day, my prayer would be answered," John said.

Without telling his wife, John dutifully said the prayer to Saint Jude over the prescribed period, but he noticed nothing different on the eighth day. Still, he figured nothing ventured, nothing gained. "I'm...flexible enough to try anything that might improve my luck or health," John said, "particularly when the newspaper classified ad sounded so convincing."

Upon returning from a vacation, John revisited his doctor and had a new blood test done. "When I called the doctor's nurse a few days later and asked for my score, she replied, 'You can be on my team anytime!'" The test revealed that John was quite healthy. Two years after his surgery, John was still in remission. "I've never felt better," he said, "and I probably appreciate and enjoy life more now than I ever have before.

"Whether my miracle occurred because of the prayers of my family and friends, medical science and high technology, or my new friend, Saint Jude," John said, "I will never know, although I suspect the latter!"

"Jerry Had a Bilateral Skull Fracture and Internal Bleeding"

"My story begins on December 10, 1975," said Cathy V. of Euclid, Ohio. "It was 10:00 P.M., I was watching television, and the telephone rang. I answered it only to hear a voice tell me that my husband, Jerry, had been in an automobile accident."

The voice on the phone was that of a nurse at the hospital Jerry was taken to. She asked Cathy for permission to treat her husband, which Cathy immediately gave, and this tipped her off that Jerry must have been hurt seriously and couldn't communicate with the medical staff.

Cathy called her sister to come and take care of the three children, ages three, four, and five, then she called a friend to drive her to the hospital. "I was told that Jerry had a bilateral skull fracture and internal bleeding," Cathy said. "He was semiconscious, which meant that he would raise his hand if they asked him to, but he could not communicate with them verbally."

Jerry was in a serious state of shock, and his condition was so critical that Cathy was asked to go to the waiting room, where she would be called if there was any change in her husband's condition. "Thoughts of prayer raced through my mind. I had always been taught to pray at these times, but for some reason I just couldn't find the words."

An hour after she arrived at the hospital, a nurse told Cathy that the doctor had performed an emergency tracheotomy on Jerry and that this had probably saved his life. A major artery to Jerry's brain, in the back of his head, had been ruptured. This caused massive bleeding that was causing him to choke. In the course of that night, Jerry would receive seven pints of blood by transfusion.

Still more "thoughts of prayer" came to Cathy, but still she could not find the words. "I didn't know how to approach God with something as important as this," she said. "Then I remembered Jerry's strong faith in Saint Jude. He told me once that Saint Jude was the saint of impossible things, and when things got really difficult for him, he would pray to Saint Jude."

Cathy decided to pray to Saint Jude on her husband's behalf. "I pleaded with him to ask our dear Lord to save Jerry's life. After several attempts at packing Jerry's nose to try to stop the bleeding, a doctor finally succeeded, and the bleeding stopped."

Medical personnel moved Jerry into the intensive-care unit. His condition was listed as stable but still critical. The next two days went by quickly, but Jerry's condition neither improved nor worsened. Then came the news that Jerry's left lung had been injured in the accident, causing it to function at only about 15 percent of its capacity. This meant that the right lung had to do its own work, plus try to compensate for the weakened left lung. Because it was being overworked, the right lung went into shock. "The doctor told me he had never seen a shocked lung come out of shock in time to do any good," Cathy said. "He suspected that Jerry would die in two or three days. He also said there was nothing more on earth that could be done for Jerry. He was in God's hands now."

Terrified, Cathy asked her brother-in-law to take her to the hospital chapel. Once there, however, she again found herself unable to pray, not knowing what to say to God. Again she decided to turn to Saint Jude. He had interceded with God and kept Jerry alive this long, so Cathy pleaded once more with Saint Jude to ask God to save her husband. "I needed him with me on earth."

As Cathy prayed, a thought came to her. She remembered the story of Lazarus, in the Gospel of John, and how Jesus brought him back to life after he was dead and buried. "Suddenly," Cathy said, "I felt very foolish. It was as though Saint Jude and our Lord were telling me that I was praying for someone who was alive, and if our Lord could bring someone back to life who had died, what did I have to fear? From that moment on, I knew Jerry would not die. I knew my prayer to our Lord through Saint Jude had been answered."

The next day, Cathy received word that her husband's condition had changed dramatically during the night. The doctor had no explanation, he simply said that now he thought Jerry would make it. He was responding well to medication and it looked like his lung was coming out of shock.

Continuing to improve, Jerry finally realized what had happened to him two weeks after the accident. Now came the news that he would need more surgery. His femur had been completely severed below the ball of the hip, and no blood had been able to reach the ball for the past two weeks. The doctors would repair the femur now, but in about ten months he would need hip replacement surgery. Otherwise he would be handicapped for life. The hip surgery was not done earlier because it was too dangerous to administer a general anesthetic while the skull fracture kept Jerry in critical condition.

The surgery to repair Jerry's femur was done on Christmas Eve. "Once again," Cathy said, "I asked Saint Jude's help. Once again, he came through for me. Jerry survived the surgery and has not had to have any additional surgery on his leg or hip. The doctors are still stunned."

January 10, 1976, one month, to the day, after his accident, Jerry returned home. The left side of his face had been paralyzed from the skull fracture. He and Cathy were told that he would require surgery to release pressure from the facial nerve because the swelling from the fracture was causing the paralysis. Within two weeks, however, the paralysis was gone.

When Jerry left the hospital, he brought along a six-month prescription for a pain-relieving medication. The doctor expected Jerry to have severe headaches due to the skull fracture. "Jerry never took one pill for a headache," Cathy said.

"On the surface," Cathy continued, "it would appear as though the miracle Jerry and I received that year was one of physical healing, but it goes much deeper than that. Jerry and I were not doing very well as a married couple. We were basically living separate lives. We were young and had so many responsibilities with our three children, and we really did not know how to cope."

Jerry, as a young husband and father, had the most difficult time. He wanted to be single again, but he didn't want to shirk his responsibilities to his wife and children. After the accident, Jerry became a different person. His family now came first in his life. "He wanted us to make it as a couple and as a family," Cathy said.

While Jerry recuperated at home, he received visits from a Catholic priest, originally from India, from the couple's parish. He brought Jerry holy Communion each day, and they had many talks together. The priest talked with Jerry about becoming a lay eucharistic minister in his parish. The priest also told Jerry about the restoration of the permanent diaconate in the Catholic Church in the United States. The priest didn't know a great deal about this ministry, but he suggested that Jerry might want to look into it.

"When Jerry became fully well," Cathy said, "he did become a eucharistic minister, and he did look into the permanent diaconate, only to learn that he was too young. You had to be at least thirty-two before you could apply for the program to become a deacon."

Years later, at age forty-three, Jerry is an ordained permanent deacon for the Catholic Diocese of Cleveland, Ohio.

"Little did I know where my prayer to Saint Jude would lead us," Cathy said. "Little did I know that by asking him to intercede for me with our Lord, Jerry would not only be granted more time on this earth, but he would also be given the gift of a calling to the permanent diaconate.

"I will always be grateful to Saint Jude. I didn't really know him until that fateful day of the accident. I know him very well now. We have become friends in prayer to God."

"I Had a Nagging Fear Something Was Wrong With the Pregnancy"

Pat R. C. of Burdett, New York, has had ongoing contact with Saint Jude, especially during difficult pregnancies. "Saint Jude first entered my life," she said, "in 1960 when I was expecting my sixth child. I had a nagging fear something was wrong with the pregnancy."

When a local parish announced a novena to Saint Jude, Pat attended and prayed for a healthy baby. Four weeks overdue, she went into labor but with no significant results. Finally, a baby girl was born, but the umbilical cord was wrapped tightly around her neck. "The doctor had to cut the cord six times, but the baby recovered quickly and grew to a fine young lady," Pat said. After the baby's birth, Pat's husband gave her a statue of Saint Jude. "With eight children, he was prayed to a lot."

In 1985, Kathleen, the baby born under such difficult circumstances in 1960, was hospitalized for appendicitis. The diagnosis, however, was more complicated. Treated with antibiotics intravenously for five days, she only grew worse. Pat prayed, "Help, Saint Jude, take care of your miracle child."

Finally, two surgeries were done for a ruptured appendix and abscesses, and Kathleen recovered. When Kathleen married, she was unable to become pregnant and underwent surgery to try to correct the problem. "Saint Jude helped," Pat said, "and my grandchild Sarah was born in 1988."

"After Twenty Years of Marriage
I Divorced My Hard-Working Husband"

Because his drinking after work was causing him to be violent, said Marina L. of San Diego, California, "after twenty years of marriage I divorced my hard-working husband. While alone with my nine-year-old daughter, I suffered heart pains constantly from sadness. I was depressed, and all day and part of the night I would cry and pray…."

Marina ate so little each day that her daughter refused to eat the little food they had unless her mother had a bite or two as well.

Almost daily, Marina went to a little nearby church "to cry to our Lord." One day as she prayed, she felt without strength and no longer knew what to say to God. "I just lowered my head, rested it on top of my arms, and let my tears run down silently, watching them fall on the clean floor by my knees."

Just then, Marina noticed a folded piece of white paper. "I'm sure it wasn't there before," she said. Through her tears Marina gazed at the little folded paper, not thinking it was of any importance. "I said in my mind to our Lord, 'Abba, what do you want me to do? Who else could I pray to if not you?'"

As she said this, Marina picked up the piece of paper, slowly opened it, and read, "Pray to Saint Jude." "Lord, if you are really telling me this," Marina thought, "then I want a sign." She went a few pews back to see a statue of Saint Jude. "I stood there…looking at his features. I said, feeling very sad, 'Saint Jude, you have a frown on your forehead right between your eyebrows just like my father, and like me…and you look angry…well, it is not your fault the artist made you look like that. Saint Jude, if our Lord really wants me to pray to you, then you must give me a novena if there is such a thing, for I have never heard about novenas for you."

Marina went to the rectory and asked the secretary there about novenas to Saint Jude. The secretary told her to come to church on Sunday and look in the back of the church where there was a library. Maybe she could find one there. Retracing her steps back to the church, Marina stood in front of Saint Jude's statue and told him, "No, I won't wait until Sunday. I won't inquire anymore. You know I'm about to cry again and can't stand this pain and sadness. Please, if you are to help me, give me your novena, and I promise to pray it."

Looking around in the church, Marina found nothing. "I was checking the pews near Saint Jude's statue for the second time when I noticed a book. I picked it up. It was his novena. I went home and said the novena to Saint Jude."

Three months later, Marina felt more and more depressed, when at midnight her husband walked in. "He stayed for good, and we...remarried," she said. "He stopped drinking for the rest of our married life, which was twelve years. He died in 1991."

"I Began to Have Flashbacks of Sexual Abuse"

As a child, Ann C. of New Hyde Park, New York, was given a card with a prayer on it to Saint Jude. "I prayed to him faithfully throughout many, many years of confusion," she said.

At the age of forty-four, Ann said, "I began to have flashbacks and memories of extensive sexual abuse until age sixteen. I know now my devotion to Saint Jude carried me through many a hopeless moment."

Ann said that her healing began when she left home at age twenty, but "the real miracles" began when she started to remember what had happened to her. "I do know that Saint Jude was there for me and was very important to my survival. He never thought I was hopeless. He cared for me as did our Lord."

"I Concentrated on 'Scoring Drugs'"

"I am and always have been gay and an addictive person," said Joe S. of Albany, New York. "Though I do not practice homosexuality anymore or partake of drugs, I was deeply involved in both. I am college educated and have risen above my troubled adolescence to carry my cross with dignity and love."

Joe was a bartender and started taking amphetamines to make it to the bar's 4:00 A.M. closing. Soon, he began taking amphetamines "for any and every reason." Thus he became aware of the drug sub-culture, and he found it fascinating. "The highs were incredible as I progressed through the various drugs including heroin and my drug of choice—cocaine."

Soon, cocaine took over Joe's life. Nothing else mattered except injecting the drug that made his life bearable. "I... concentrated on 'scoring drugs.'"

Eventually, Joe was arrested, and he "cleaned up his act" by, he said, "isolating myself in the woods for seven months." During this time, Joe began to remember the wonderful feelings he had from growing up in the Catholic religion. "A product of fairly well-off parents, and the youngest of four boys, Church played an important part in my early life. As I thought about it, I realized how low my life had become—stealing, lying, sleeping in doorways, and so on."

Joe found his way back to a healthy life and a good job. He stayed "clean" for twelve years. Then one night he was out drinking and met an old classmate and his girlfriend. "I invited them to 'crash' at my apartment," Joe said. "The next morning when they did not come to the kitchen, and knowing they had to leave for their hometown soon, I went into their room. They were fine, but there on the nightstand was a needle and that beautiful white powder.

"Everything [else] in my life no longer mattered," Joe

continued. "I quickly injected and my hell began anew. After three years of this, and being back on the bottom of the heap of life, I tried to quit again. Though I knew I wasn't worthy, I went to our church and began to pray. Suddenly, the tears flowed heavily. When I opened my eyes again there on the pew in front of me was a novena card to Saint Jude."

Beginning a novena to Saint Jude, Joe visited with a Catholic priest a few weeks later and began to attend daily Mass. He is now "clean" and has been since 1986. Joe participated in a drug rehabilitation program, but always maintained his novena to Saint Jude for, he said, "the wonderful miracle he did by getting me through each day."

Joe added that in his drug-abuse days, he and three others used to get together daily and share needles. "The three others have all died of AIDS. I get tested regularly, but my physician says that miraculously I am free of the disease and at this point probably will stay free."

Today, Joe said, he is "a respected member of my church and community. Saint Jude's statue remains in my bedroom. The thoughts of my hell, my cross, will always be with me, along with the glory of Saint Jude."

"I Prayed That My Baby Would Be Born Healthy"

When Patricia C. of Brentwood, New York, was nineteen years old, she was expecting her first child. Suddenly, seven months into the pregnancy, she was taken to a hospital emergency room, paralyzed. She almost died from complications due to poliomyelitis.

"Prayers and petitions were sent to Saint Jude," Patricia said, "and candles were lighted. I prayed that my baby would be born healthy. Two months later, I had a wonderful, healthy baby boy."

"My Request Was to Pass an Exam..."

Following a novena to Saint Jude, Rose Mary G. of Albuquerque, New Mexico, asked Saint Jude to help her pass an exam and, ultimately, a class in organic chemistry she was taking in school. "My own efforts, to date, had been woefully inadequate. I had been unable to even get a D when I took the class previously, so I was repeating it. This course is a prerequisite for medical school."

On the two previous exams, Rose Mary received a 69 and a 30, despite disciplined study. She needed at least a C to pass the course.

Unfortunately, several crises and conflicting obligations happened during the weeks prior to the third exam, and Rose Mary was able to study for only two days. "The result of my prayers to Saint Jude was that I earned a 71 on the third exam, the exact grade I needed to maintain a 70 average. [Students were allowed to drop one grade.]

"I am so grateful for Saint Jude's intercession," Rose Mary said.

"I Was Told That My Job Would Be Terminated"

Diane J. of Sunnyside, New York, had been working for the same company for forty years, but in January 1992, she found out that her company was moving to Raleigh, North Carolina. "I was told that my job would be terminated in May 1992," she said. "I was not asked to move to North Carolina. I was very upset." Diane felt that because of her age (she was fifty-seven at the time), her lack of experience with computers, and the slow economy and high unemployment, she would have a terrible time finding another job.

"I began praying to Saint Jude for help," Diane said. "I asked that somehow I would be allowed to keep my job or for help in finding a new one. Saint Jude helped in a very special way." Two weeks before her company was to move, Diane and her supervisor were called into the president's office and told that they would be staying on a temporary basis until suitable replacements could be hired. "My company rented us an office in a nearby town...equipped us with a word-processing typewriter, copy machine, fax machine, answering machine, postage machine, and so on, so that we were self-sufficient. We were told that we would be there about six months...or until they found replacements."

On May 15, 1992, Diane and her supervisor moved into their new office...and are *still there*. "They have not found replacements for us," Diane said. "They came very close once, but again, I prayed to Saint Jude, and the persons they were planning to hire decided not to take the job."

Diane and her supervisor were informed that they could remain in their jobs until they are ready to leave. "My supervisor is nearing retirement age and he has been told that it is up to him when he wants to leave. I am now almost sixty and I am hoping for at least two to three more years. I know, with Saint Jude's help, I will get my wish."

"My Husband Had a Heart Attack"

Kathryn G. of Haddon Heights, New Jersey, said: "My husband had a heart attack and went into cardiac arrest. I was devastated."

Praying to Saint Jude, Kathryn asked for her husband's life to be spared. "My husband recovered," she said, "and lived for fifteen years after that horrible day."

"I Had No Idea How Miserable and Unhappy She Had Been"

Maria F. of Brooklyn, New York, said that her devotion to Saint Jude began in 1966 when her father underwent surgery for colon cancer. She prayed to Saint Jude for her father, and he lived ten more years after the surgery.

After college graduation, Maria's best friend went to graduate school, attending a school in the southeast part of the United States. "She came home for summer break, but I had no idea how miserable and unhappy she had been."

The night before Maria's friend was to return to graduate school, she called Maria and told her with many tears of her unhappiness. "She dreaded going back and was almost in a panic."

Maria promised she would pray to Saint Jude for her friend. "Two nights later, she called me," Maria said. Her friend had already returned to school and come back home. As soon as she arrived back at school, the chairman of the department called for her. He told her that he and the faculty knew how unhappy she had been. They devised an alternative plan that would allow Maria's friend to finish her studies at home and still earn her master's degree.

"He Could Have Been a Defendant in Over Three Hundred Lawsuits"

Maria F. of the preceding story has a cousin who is an assistant district attorney in Arizona. He asked Maria to pray for a special favor, so Maria began a novena to Saint Jude for her cousin.

"About seven days later," Maria said, "he called to tell me his prayer had been answered. The Supreme Court was hearing an appeal [regarding] a state law. If it ruled against the district attorney's office, he would have been personally liable.... He could have been a defendant in over three hundred [lawsuits] by people he had prosecuted. It looked very bad, [but] the next day—about seven days into the novena— the judge ruled for the state. My cousin called immediately to tell me."

"The Corneas Were Burned Off Both Eyes"

"It was a warm evening in April 1978," said Lillian C. of Albany, New York, "and my husband, Jack, had come home with a rental car he was to drive to a business meeting in another city the next day."

Jack said that the windshield of the rental car was covered with deceased bugs. Could she please wash the windshield for him? Lillian took out a bottle of household ammonia and poured some in a basin. Ordinarily, she would put water in the basin first, then add ammonia so there would never be undiluted ammonia in an open container. This time, without thinking, she did the reverse.

"As I placed the basin under the faucet," Lillian recalled, "I hit the faucet and the ammonia splashed out of the basin all over the front of me. It took my breath away, so I ran to the door to breathe in some fresh air."

Jack, realizing what had happened, grabbed Lillian and pulled her back to the sink and began pouring water on her face. When the water hit the ammonia the fumes increased, and Lillian tugged away from her husband and ran back to the door. Again Jack got his wife back to the sink and began pouring water in her face. Lillian told him he had better call an ambulance as she knew that ammonia causes caustic burns, and the caustic burns would continue to burn even after the ammonia was washed away.

When Jack phoned for an ambulance, the call went out over the mobile radio system used by police and firefighters, and a fireman who lives down the street from Jack and Lillian heard it. He rushed to their house to help and asked Lillian if she had swallowed any ammonia, but she didn't know. Just in case, the fireman had Lillian drink a glass of milk.

The ambulance arrived, and all the way to the hospital the emergency medical crew continued to irrigate Lillian's eyes. They also radioed to the hospital that they were bringing in a woman with caustic burns.

At the hospital, the medical personnel went into action. "For hours," Lillian said, "they continued to pour water on my face and irrigate my eyes. As I waited for x-rays of my lungs I began to pray to Saint Jude. 'Please let me be okay, and please don't let me be blind. I have two young children.'"

The x-ray report indicated no damage to Lillian's lungs, but the news was not so good on her eyes. The corneas were burned off of both eyes, and there were burns on the sclera—the white part—of her right eye. "There was definite damage."

Lillian put her finger inside her lower lip and peeled out burned skin. Her face had first-degree burns, and she was in pain. "I continued to pray to Saint Jude," she said. "My parish priest and a prayer group prayed. My family and friends prayed."

The doctor said that Lillian's corneas should grow back, but there was permanent damage to the sclera in the right eye. She couldn't see the big E on the eye chart at all.

"The corneas began to grow back," Lillian said, "feeling like constant sand under my eyelids. I couldn't stand bright light and wore wraparound sunglasses day and night. Prayers continued."

At the end of May, Lillian went back for another examination by her doctor. "He looked, and finally he turned the examination light off and sat back in his chair. I never prayed so hard in all my life, and finally I said to Saint Jude, 'Help me be strong enough to accept what I have to hear.'"

The doctor told Lillian he couldn't understand it. "There was no sign of scarring, no damage to the sclera, and the corneas had completely grown back. He said that if he hadn't seen me before he would never have known that my eyes were burned so badly. The eye test showed 20-20 vision. He couldn't believe it, as caustic burns are very difficult to heal, and almost always leave severe damage."

The doctor told Lillian she was very lucky, but, she said, "I knew better. I truly felt it was the power of prayer and Saint Jude had answered those prayers."

She Lost Her Voice and Couldn't Sing

At age seventy-three, during the winter of 1993, Agnes R. of Camden, New Jersey, lost her voice. "Singing, especially at Mass, was impossible," she said. "Did it worry me? Of course. I hadn't had a cold for thirty years [that] required medical attention."

Agnes recalled the many times, earlier in life, when she had called on Saint Jude for help when her young children were sick. She prayed to Saint Jude. "He obtained the healing," she said. "I can now sing like before, and maybe better at times."

For Many Years She Tried to Conceive a Child

"My daughter," said Mrs. Francis L. of Hollywood, Florida, "tried for many years to conceive a child, and she went to many doctors. Finally, in 1992 she became pregnant."

Mrs. L. said that she "prayed every day, nine times a day, to Saint Jude for my daughter to have a safe delivery and a healthy child." In 1993, at the age of forty-one, Mrs. L.'s daughter gave birth, and she and her husband became the parents of a beautiful baby girl.

"I Had Arthritis in My Arm From Shoulder to Hand"

Jennie M. of Elmont, New York, said that at the end of 1993 she had had arthritis in her arm "from shoulder to hand." Then she started to feel arthritis in her other arm, too.

A friend gave Mrs. M. a small bottle of Saint Jude blessed oil and a prayer to Saint Jude to say when applying the blessed oil. "I said it with all my heart," Mrs. M. said, "and Saint Jude answered my prayer. I swear to it, I have no pain in my arm, and it's almost gone in my other arm."

He Wanted to Be With His Wife
When Their Baby Was Born

During the Korean conflict, in the early 1950s, Leonard P. of Melrose, Massachusetts, was called to active duty as a reserve officer in the U.S. Army Corps of Engineers. In July 1952, he was assigned to Korea with fourteen months left of his two-year active duty commitment. "At that time," he said, "my wife, Rosemary, was expecting our second child, due in about four months.

"[We] shared a deep desire that I be present in November when our baby was to be born," he said, "but that possibility seemed hopeless."

All the same, before Leonard left for Korea he gave Rosemary a Saint Jude prayer card. He suggested that they both pray to Saint Jude to intercede on their behalf to get him home for their child's birth. "As a matter of fact," Leonard said, "I made the irrational promise that I would be home for the big moment."

Leonard and Rosemary both "prayed fervently" and shared the progress of the pregnancy in frequent letters.

In later October 1952, "from out of the blue," Leonard said, an order came from Washington, D.C., announcing that all reserve officers with previous military service were eligible for immediate discharge. Since Leonard had served in the U.S. Navy for two years during World War II, his commanding officer agreed that he was, indeed, eligible for discharge. "After learning of my special circumstances, he expedited the cutting of my release orders," Leonard said.

Excited to be heading home, Leonard still wondered if he would make it back in time for the baby's birth. "As soon as my release was confirmed," he said, "I mailed a Special Delivery letter to Rosemary with the good news. I learned later that she received the letter on October 28, the feast day of Saint Jude. And she learned later that I left Korea on a troopship on, yes, October 28."

After a few days in Japan and fifteen days on aboard ship, Leonard arrived in San Francisco on November 14. A telephone call revealed that he was not too late—not yet, at least. The fastest route to Boston required a flight to New York and an overnight train ride to Boston. The train arrived at South Station in Boston, at about 6:30 A.M. Sunday, November 16. "My beautiful pregnant wife and my grateful parents were there to greet me," Leonard recalled. "Our prayers were answered."

On the way home, the timing was right for Leonard and his family to attend the early Mass at their parish church. "We should not have been surprised to hear the postcommunion reading of the words of Jesus from Saint Mark's Gospel," Leonard said: "So I tell you, whatever you ask for in prayer, believe that you have received it, and it will be yours" (11:24).

Mark Edward was born on Monday morning, November 17.

"His Wallet Had Fallen Into the Lake"

In 1985, Ann D. of Antioch, Illinois, and her extended family were vacationing in the northern highlands of Wisconsin, camping out and sleeping in tents. "My mom and dad were able to join us for a week," she said, "and so lots of hiking, canoeing, and, of course, fishing were on the agenda."

One evening, Ann's father was out fishing in the canoe with Ann's husband, Tom. Ann recalled the long face on her father when they returned. "It was unusual, because he was always smiling and cheering others up. But not tonight."

Ann's father explained, with tears in his eyes, that he had been sitting in the back of the canoe, and "sometime during the course of that evening outing his wallet, containing all of his money for that trip, had fallen into the lake."

After Ann's father had calmed down a bit, he gathered everyone around and asked them all to pray to Saint Jude, which they all did, feeling very helpless.

"Dad's an early riser," Ann said, "and so by the time we all got up the next morning, he had taken off. As he was to explain later, he had a dream that night that showed the exact spot the wallet fell in. So when he awoke he was surely anxious to seek out this spot, while it was clear in his memory."

The wallet lay submerged in only four feet of the clearest lake water imaginable. "We thanked the Lord and Saint Jude," Ann said, "and after we helped lay out and dry all his wet money, driver's license, and so forth, Dad treated us all to huge ice-cream cones."

"I Had to Pray for Friends"

Linda K. of Lake Ronkonkoma, New York, said that there was a time in her life when she turned to Saint Jude for help in finding some friends. "Looking back," she said, "that seems so sad, to have to pray to find friends."

As a young teenager, Linda said, she was "falling in with a bad crowd, but they were better than having no friends at all. School was so hard, because everyone was in a clique or group. I would cry all the time, and was very depressed."

Linda prayed a novena to Saint Jude for one week, asking him to lead her to some good friends. "The miracle answer to my prayers is in full force up to today," Linda said. "My two best friends I met my first year in high school, and we continue to be the best of friends, even though we are separated by many miles. We are all married with children of our own."

Saint Jude, Linda said, led her to good friends that have had a long-lasting effect on her life. "My later teen years and my young adult years took such a happy turn of events because of these two friends. As I look at my own children, they are still young, but as they approach adolescence I am very aware of their friendships and their lives, and that novena to Saint Jude is always in the back of my mind. Maybe I can make it for my children—although I will have to pray to Saint Anthony to find it!"

"I Got a Big Lump in My Jaw in the Parotid Gland"

Joyce D. of Copiague, New York, said that she has an incurable disease which results in no saliva and no tears in her eyes. "I got a big lump in the parotid gland in my jaw and it was there for one year."

Joyce underwent many tests and saw several doctors, and the lump in her jaw did not prove to be malignant. Finally, a dental surgeon advised an operation. "This would be a very delicate and dangerous operation, and the doctor would have to cut nerves in my face, which would make one side of my face move up, and it would take a long time to get any feeling back in my face, if ever. My jaw could become paralyzed permanently."

The doctor insisted that this surgery was necessary, but Joyce said that she wanted to wait. "I started novenas to Saint Jude and Saint Anthony," she said. "I had been praying for one year already, but nothing had happened." Then on November 21, 1993, Joyce and her husband attended Mass together. "During Mass, I said to my husband, 'Guess what? I don't feel that lump in my jaw.' My husband put his hand on my jaw and said, 'I don't believe it. It's not there.' I knew my prayers were heard."

Four months later, the lump was still gone from Joyce's jaw, and her doctor had no explanation.

Before They Could Build a School, They Had to Have Sisters

"When I was a boy—roughly eleven or twelve years old," said Father Mike M. of Miami, Florida, "—we lived in Brandon, Florida, a few miles east of Tampa. Our parish wanted to build a school, but before we could do so we had to have Sisters to teach in it. This was about 1960."

Father M. said that his family turned to Saint Jude. Each evening as part of his family's night prayers, the family of mother, father, and three children assembled. "We included a special prayer to Saint Jude that we would get Sisters so we could build a parish school. It seemed like a couple of years we did this, but for certain it was a long time."

The pastor of the parish got one refusal after another from various congregations of nuns. Finally, the Trinitarian Sisters said yes, and the first classrooms were built, plus a convent, "and the Sisters came."

Years later, Father M. said, the Sisters withdrew, but the school continues to flourish, thanks to Saint Jude.

Prayers and Novenas to

SAINT ANTHONY
and
SAINT JUDE

Prayer for Lost Objects

Saint Anthony,
when you prayed your stolen book of prayers
was returned to you.
Pray now for all of us who have lost things
precious and dear.
Pray for all who have lost faith, hope,
or the friendship of God.
Pray for us who have lost friends or relatives by death.
Pray for all who have lost peace of mind or spirit.
Pray that we may be given new hope, new faith, new love.
Pray that lost things, needful and helpful to us,
may be returned to our keeping.
Or, if we must continue in our loss, pray that we may be
granted Christ's comfort and peace

(mention petition).
Amen.

Unfailing Prayer to Saint Anthony

O holy Saint Anthony,
gentlest of saints, your love for God
and charity for his creatures,
made you worthy, when on earth,
to possess miraculous powers.

Miracles waited on your word,
which you were ever ready to speak
for those in trouble or anxiety.
Encouraged by this thought,
I implore you to obtain for me

(mention request).

The answer to my prayer may
require a miracle, even so,
you are the Saint of Miracles.

O gentle and loving Saint Anthony,
whose heart was ever full of human sympathy,
whisper my petition into the ears
of the Sweet Infant Jesus,
who loved to be folded in your arms;
and the gratitude of my heart
will ever be yours.
Amen.

Tribute to Saint Anthony of Padua

Good Saint Anthony, in God's providence
you have secured for all his people
many marvelous favors.
You have been especially celebrated
for your goodness to the poor and the hungry,
for finding employment for those seeking it,
for your special care of those who travel,
and for keeping safe from harm
all who must be away from home.

You are widely known also,
good Saint Anthony,
for securing peace in the family,
for your delicate mercy in finding lost things,
for safe delivery of messages,
and for your concern for women in childbirth.

In honoring you, Saint Anthony,
for the many graces our Lord grants through your favor,
we trustfully and confidently ask
your aid in our present need.

V. Pray for us, Saint Anthony.
R. That we may be made worth of the promise of Christ.

Let us pray:

May it be a source of joy to your Church, O God,
that we honor the memory of your confessor and doctor,
Saint Anthony.
May his spiritual help always make us strong,
and, by his assistance, may we enjoy an eternal reward.
This we ask through Jesus Christ, our Lord. Amen.

The Saint Anthony Novena Prayer

O wonderful Saint Anthony,
glorious on account of the fame of your miracles,
and through the condescension of Jesus
in coming in the form of a little child
to rest in your arms,
obtain for me of his bounty
the grace which I ardently desire
from the depths of my heart

(mention request).
You who were so compassionate toward miserable sinners,
regard not the unworthiness of those who pray to you,
but the glory of God
that it may once again be magnified
by the granting of the particular request
which I now ask for with persevering earnestness.

*(Say one Our Father, one Hail Mary, and
one Glory Be in honor of Saint Anthony.)*
Saint Anthony, pray for us.
Amen.

The Nine-Day Novena to Saint Anthony

DAY ONE

O holy Saint Anthony, gentlest of saints,
your love for God and charity for his creatures,
made you worthy, when on earth,
to possess miraculous powers.
Miracles waited on your word,
which you were ever ready to speak for those
in trouble or anxiety.
Encouraged by this thought,
I implore you to obtain for me

(mention request).

The answer to my prayer may require a miracle,
even so, you are the Saint of Miracles.
O gentle and loving Saint Anthony,
whose heart was ever full of human sympathy,
whisper my petition into the ears of the Sweet Infant Jesus,
who loved to be folded in your arms;
and the gratitude of my heart will ever be yours.

*(Say one Our Father, one Hail Mary,
and one Glory Be in honor of Saint Anthony.)*

Saint Anthony, pray for us.

Amen.

DAY TWO

O miracle-working Saint Anthony,
remember that it never has been heard that you left
without help or relief anyone in need
who had recourse to you.
Animated now with the most lively confidence,
even with full conviction of not being refused,

I fly for refuge to you,
O most favored friend of the Infant Jesus.
O eloquent preacher of the divine mercy,
despise not my supplications but,
bringing them before the throne of God,
strengthen them by your intercession and
obtain for me the favor I seek in this novena

(mention request).
(Say one Our Father, one Hail Mary,
and one Glory Be in honor of Saint Anthony.)
Saint Anthony, pray for us.
Amen.

DAY THREE

O purest Saint Anthony,
who through your angelic virtue was made
worthy to be caressed by the Divine Child Jesus,
to hold him in your arms and press him to your heart.
I entreat you to cast a benevolent glance upon me.
O glorious Saint Anthony,
born under the protection of Mary Immaculate,
on the feast of her Assumption into heaven,
and consecrated to her and now so powerful
an intercessor in heaven,
I beseech you to obtain for me the favor
I ask in this novena

(mention request).
O great wonder-worker,
intercede for me that God may grant my request.

(Say one Our Father, one Hail Mary,
and one Glory Be in honor of Saint Anthony.)
Saint Anthony, pray for us.
Amen.

DAY FOUR

I salute and honor you, O powerful helper, Saint Anthony.
The Christian world confidently turns to you and
experiences your tender compassion and powerful
assistance in so many necessities and sufferings
that I am encouraged in my need to seek your help
in obtaining a favorable answer
to my request for the favor I seek in this novena

(mention request).

O holy Saint Anthony, I beseech you,
obtain for me the grace that I desire.

*(Say one Our Father, one Hail Mary,
and one Glory Be in honor of Saint Anthony.)*

Saint Anthony, pray for us.

Amen.

DAY FIVE

I salute you, Saint Anthony, lily of purity,
ornament and glory of Christianity.
I salute you, great Saint,
cherub of wisdom and seraph of divine love.
I rejoice at the favors our Lord has
so liberally bestowed upon you.
In humility and confidence I entreat you to help me,
for I know that God has given you charity and pity,
as well as power.
I ask you by the love you did feel toward the
Infant Jesus as you held him in your arms
to tell him now of the favor I seek through
your intercession in this novena

(mention request).

(Say one Our Father, one Hail Mary,
and one Glory Be in honor of Saint Anthony.)
Saint Anthony, pray for us.
Amen.

DAY SIX

O glorious Saint Anthony,
chosen by God to preach his Word,
you received from him the gift of tongues and
the power of working the most extraordinary miracles.
O good Saint Anthony,
pray that I may fulfill the will of God in all things
so that I may love him, with you, for all eternity.
O kind Saint Anthony, I beseech you,
obtain for me the grace that I desire,
the favor I seek in this novena

(mention request).

(Say one Our Father, one Hail Mary,
and one Glory Be in honor of Saint Anthony.)
Saint Anthony, pray for us.
Amen.

DAY SEVEN

O renowned champion of the faith of Christ,
most holy Saint Anthony, glorious for your many miracles,
obtain for me from the bounty of my Lord and God
the grace which I ardently seek in this novena

(mention request).

O holy Saint Anthony, ever attentive to those who invoke you,
grant me that aid of your powerful intercession.

(Say one Our Father, one Hail Mary,
and one Glory Be in honor of Saint Anthony.)
Saint Anthony, pray for us.
Amen.

DAY EIGHT

O holy Saint Anthony,
you have shown yourself so powerful in your intercession,
so tender and so compassionate towards those
who honor you and invoke you in suffering and distress.
I beseech you most humbly and earnestly
to take me under your protection
in my present necessities and to obtain for me
the favor I desire

(mention request).
Recommend my request to the merciful Queen of Heaven,
that she may plead my cause with you
before the throne of her Divine Son.

(Say one Our Father, one Hail Mary,
and one Glory Be in honor of Saint Anthony.)
Saint Anthony, pray for us.
Amen.

DAY NINE

Saint Anthony, servant of Mary,
glory of the Church, pray for our Holy Father,
our bishops, our priests, our religious orders,
that, through their pious zeal and apostolic labors,
all may be united in faith and give greater glory to God.
Saint Anthony, helper of all who invoke you,
pray for me and intercede for me before the

throne of Almighty God that I be granted the favor
I so earnestly seek in this novena

(mention request).

*(Say one Our Father, one Hail Mary,
and one Glory Be in honor of Saint Anthony.)*
Saint Anthony, pray for us.

May the divine assistance remain always with us. Amen.
May the souls of the faithful departed,
through the mercy of God, rest in peace. Amen.
O God, may the votive commemoration of blessed
Anthony, your confessor,
be a source of joy to your Church,
that she may always be fortified with spiritual assistance,
and deserve to enjoy eternal rewards.
Through Christ our Lord.
Amen.

Daily Prayer to Saint Jude

O glorious apostle, Saint Jude,
true relative of Jesus and Mary,
I salute you through the Most Sacred Heart of Jesus.
I praise and thank God for all the graces
he has bestowed upon you.
I implore you, through the Sacred Heart of Jesus,
to look upon me with compassion,
despise not my poor prayer and let not my trust be in vain.
To you has been assigned the privilege of
aiding us in the most desperate cases.
Come to my aid that I may praise the mercies of God.
All my life, I will be grateful to you
and will be your faithful client
until I can thank you in heaven.
Amen.

Prayer for Consolation and Help in Time of Despair

Most holy Apostle Saint Jude,
faithful servant and friend of Jesus,
the name of the traitor who delivered the beloved Master
into the hands of his enemies
has caused you to be forgotten by many,
but the Church honors and invokes you universally
as the patron of hopeless cases,
of things almost despaired of.
Pray for me, I am so helpless and alone.
Make use, I implore you,
of that particular privilege given to you,
to bring visible and speedy help,
where help is almost despaired of.
Come to my assistance in this great need,
that I may receive the consolations and help of heaven
in all my necessities, tribulations, and sufferings,
particularly...

(mention request),
and that I may bless God with you
and all the elect forever.
I promise, O blessed Saint Jude,
to be ever mindful of this great favor,
to always honor you
as my special and powerful patron,
and to gratefully encourage devotion to you.
Amen.

Prayer for a Patient

Dear Apostle and Martyr for Christ,
you left us an Epistle in the New Testament.
With good reason many invoke you
when illness is at a desperate stage.
We now recommend to your kindness...

(name of patient),
who is in a critical condition.
May the cure of this patient increase
his/her faith and love for the Lord of Life,
for the glory of our merciful God.
Amen.

The Saint Jude Novena Prayer

To Saint Jude, Holy Saint Jude, Apostle and Martyr,
great in virtue and rich in miracles,
near kinsman of Jesus Christ,
faithful intercessor of all who invoke your
special patronage in time of need.
To you I have recourse from the depths of my heart
and humbly beg to whom God has given
such great power to come to my assistance.
Help me in my present and urgent petition;
in return I promise to make your name known
and cause you to be invoked.
Saint Jude pray for us and all who invoke your aid.

*(Say one Our Father, one Hail Mary,
and one Glory Be in honor of Saint Anthony.)*
Amen.

Nine-Day Novena to Saint Jude

DAY ONE

O blessed apostle Saint Jude,
who labored zealously among the Gentiles in many lands,
and performed numerous miracles
in needy and despairing cases,
we invoke you to take special interest in us and our needs.
We feel that you understand us in a particular way.
Hear our prayers and our petitions and plead
for us in all our necessities, especially…

(mention request).
May we be patient in learning God's holy will and
courageous in carrying it out.
Amen.
Saint Jude, pray for us! My Jesus, mercy!

DAY TWO

O blessed apostle Jude, who has been instrumental
in gathering us here together this day,
grant that we may always serve Jesus Christ as
he deserves to be served,
giving of our best efforts in living as he wishes us to live.
May we dispose our hearts and minds that
God will always be inclined to listen
to our prayers and petitions,
especially those petitions which we
entrust to your care and for which
we ask you to plead for us

(mention request).

Grant that we may be enlightened as to what is best for us,
in the present and future,
not forgetting the blessings we have received in the past.
Amen.
Saint Jude, pray for us! My Jesus, mercy!

DAY THREE

O holy Saint Jude, apostle of Jesus Christ,
you who have so faithfully and devotedly helped
to spread his Gospel of Light,
we who are gathered together today in your honor,
ask and petition you to remember us and our needs.
Especially do we pray for...

(mention request).
May it also please our Lord to lend an ear to your
supplications on our behalf.
Grant that we may ever pray with fervor and devotion,
resigning ourselves humbly to the divine will,
seeing God's purpose in all our trials and knowing that he
will leave no sincere prayer unanswered in some way.
Amen.
Saint Jude, pray for us! My Jesus, mercy!

DAY FOUR

Blessed Saint Jude, you were
called to be one of Christ's chosen apostles and labored to
bring men to a knowledge and love of God;
listen with compassion to those gathered together to honor
you who ask your intercession.
In this troubled world of ours we have many trials,
difficulties, and temptations.
Plead for us in the heavenly court,

asking that our petitions may be answered,
especially the particular one we have
in mind at this moment

(mention request).

May it please God to answer our prayers
in the way that he knows best,
giving us grace to see his purpose in all things.

Amen.

Saint Jude, pray for us! My Jesus, mercy!

DAY FIVE

O holy Saint Jude, apostle and companion of Christ Jesus,
you have shown us by example how
to lead a life of zeal and devotion.
We humbly entreat you today to hear
our prayers and petitions.
Especially do we ask you to obtain for us
the following favor...

(mention request).

Grant that in praying for present and future
favors we may not forget the innumerable ones
granted in the past but often return to give thanks.
Humbly we resign ourselves to God's holy will,
knowing that he alone knows what
is best for us especially in our present needs and necessities.

Amen.

Saint Jude, pray for us! My Jesus, mercy!

DAY SIX

Saint Jude, apostle of Christ and helper in despairing cases,
hear the prayers and petitions of those who
are gathered together in your honor.
In all our needs and desires may we only seek what is
pleasing to God and what is best for our salvation.
These, our petitions

(mention request),

we submit to you,
asking you to obtain them for us,
if they are for the good of our souls.
We are resigned to God's holy will in all things,
knowing that he will leave no sincere prayer
unanswered in some way though it may be answered
in a way unexpected by us.
Amen.
Saint Jude, pray for us! My Jesus, mercy!

DAY SEVEN

O holy apostle Saint Jude,
in whose honor we are gathered today,
may we never forget that our Lord and Savior Jesus Christ
chose you to be one of Twelve Apostles.
Because of this and of the martyrdom
you suffered for the Faith,
we know you are a close friend of Almighty God.
Therefore we do not hesitate to petition you in our
necessities, especially…

(mention request).

We humbly submit ourselves to the will of God,
knowing full well that no sincere prayer
is ever left unanswered.

May we see God's good and gracious purpose
working in all our trials.
Amen.
Saint Jude, pray for us! My Jesus, mercy!

DAY EIGHT

O holy Saint Jude, apostle of Christ,
pray that we may ever imitate the Divine Master
and live according to his will.
May we cooperate with the grace of God and
ever remain pleasing in his sight.
Especially do we ask you to plead for us and obtain
whatsoever is necessary for our salvation.
Forget not our special petitions...

(make request).

May we always be thankful to God for the blessings we
have received in the past.
Whatsoever we ask for the present or future,
we submit to the divine will,
realizing that God knows best what is good for us.
We know he will respond to our prayers and
petitions in one way or another.
Amen.
Saint Jude, pray for us! My Jesus, mercy!

DAY NINE

O holy Saint Jude, apostle and martyr,
grant that we may so dispose our lives that
we may always be pleasing to God.
In working out our salvation in this life we have many
needs and necessities.

Today we turn to you,
asking you to intercede for us and obtain for us
the favors we ask of God.
Especially do we petition for...

(mention request).

May we not so much seek temporal good but
rather what will avail our souls,
knowing that it will profit us nothing if
we gain the whole world yet suffer the loss of our soul.
Therefore, may we incline ourselves toward the divine will,
seeing God's good and gracious purpose in all our trials.

Amen.

Saint Jude, pray for us! My Jesus, mercy!